Writing
The Great American
Romance
Novel

—

Catherine Lanigan

ALLWORTH PRESS
NEW YORK

DEDICATION

For my beloved granddaughter, Caylin. This is my legacy to you.
Should there be a time in your life when you decide you want to write a romance
novel and I am not around to help, this would be my guidance.

10 09 08 07 06   5 4 3 2 1

Published by Allworth Press
An imprint of Allworth Communications, Inc.
10 East 23rd Street, New York, NY 10010

Cover design by Derek Bacchus
Interior design by Mary Belibasakis
Page composition/typography by Integra Software Services, Pvt. Ltd., Pondicherry, India

ISBN-13: 978-1-58115-455-9
ISBN-10: 1-58115-455-0

Library of Congress Cataloging-in-Publication Data:

Lanigan, Catherine.
  Writing the great American romance novel/Catherine Lanigan.
     p. cm.
  Includes index.
  ISBN-13: 978-1-58115-455-9 (pbk.)
  ISBN-10: 1-58115-455-0 (pbk.)
  1. Love stories—Authorship. I. Title.

  PN3377.5.L68L36 2006
  808.3'85—dc22

                                                    2006016402

Printed in Canada

APPRECIATION

*M*y deepest gratitude to Lissy Peace, CEO of Blanco and Peace, who introduced me to my new publishing family at Allworth Press. Without your interception this legacy to my granddaughter might never have been shared with her and all the aspiring romantic souls who have a story to tell.

Many thanks to Tad Crawford, my publisher at Allworth, for believing in me and giving this book wings. My appreciation also goes to Jessica Rozler, my editor, whose capable hands helped to polish this stone to its intended brilliance. Thanks as well to Nana Greller of Allworth's publicity department, who concurs with me that selling this book is just as important as writing it.

A book like this is a compilation of personal and professional experiences that money cannot buy, and time will not allow all such stories to be told. I have had many who have encouraged me along the way, and some have been stars of inspiration. For this humble writer, my teachers, many of whom have passed on, taught me to envision my future and that living the life of a scholar was a noble one. Sister Dorothy Smith, my college professor and head of the English Department at Nazareth College and who died in 2005, will always be that quiet encouraging voice in my head that never lets me abandon my novel writing. My high school English teachers, Mr. Shannon Reffett, Mrs. Jo Morgan Thornburg, Mr. Linneman, Mary Ellen McCain, Dorothy MacDonald, and Gert Vernkis (who, though not a teacher, taught me a great deal): whether on this side of paradise or the other, your encouragement rings loudly.

I also want to thank my agents both past and present who have continued to support my talent and become something more valuable in my life; you are my friends. Kathy Robbins of the Robbins Agency; Mitch Douglas of ICM; Kimberley Cameron of Reese Halsey Agency; Charlotte Breeze of CDB Literary Management; and, currently, Nancy Yost and Julie Culver of Lowenstein and

Yost; Vicki McCarty of Flutie Entertainment; and Dean Schramm of the Jim Preminger Agency; and Jodee Blanco, publicist extraordinaire.

I owe much gratitude to the editors in my life who are my partners in collaboration and, at so many times, the electrical spark in my brain that I would call "inspiration." At Avon: Page Cuddy Ashley and Ellen Edwards; at MIRA/Harlequin: Dianne Moggy, Amy Moore, Martha Keenan, and Karen Taylor-Richman; at Dorchester: Alicia Condon; at HCI: Peter Vegso, Alison Janse, Matthew Diener, and Amy Hughes.

And to my family: my son, Ryan Pieszchala, and my daughter-in-law, Christy Pieszchala; my mother, Dorothy Lanigan; my brother, Ed Lanigan, and my sister-in-law, Mary Lanigan; my sister, Nancy Lanigan Porter, and my brother-in-law, David Porter; my brother, Bob Lanigan, and my sister-in-law, Debbie Lanigan; all my nieces, Karen Lanigan Jaworski, Elaine Porter Perez, Elizabeth Lanigan, Meghan Lanigan, Maureen Lanigan, Cathleen Lanigan; and my nephews, Ben Porter and Sam Porter; and my sister-in-law, Susie Garrison. I thank you all from the bottom of my heart for your patience and love as I navigate this writer's life.

And to Jed Nolan, my husband, my partner in life and in our careers. Your unswerving faith in me and in my writing sustains me every moment of the day. Your encouragement is more than just words; it is a song to my heart.

You have all been angels to me. No one could ask for more.

TABLE OF CONTENTS

*O*f all the themes in literature, poems, and song, it is love that has defied definition. Love is the one emotion that makes the human become divine. In the quest for perfect love, men and women have gone to war for love, died for love, healed themselves through love, conquered kingdoms in the name of love, and the most enterprising of souls have hired writers to immortalize their love. The modern novel format, as we know it, began in the mid-eighteenth century (1749) with the novel *Tom Jones*, by Henry Fielding. It is interesting that when Henry sat down to write, he chose romance as a theme.

Centuries have passed since then, and today, the reading public still craves the romantic novel.

In the world of publishing, the romance market is the mainstay for many publishing houses. Last year, the Association of American Publishers reported that U.S. book sales totaled $26,874,100,000 in 2002, a 5.5 percent increase over the previous year. Of that total, 1.2 billion dollars was in "mass-market" or rack-size paperbacks. Historically, paperback romance sales have averaged no less than 51 percent of the 1.2-billion-dollar paperback sales, thus dominating the paperback market more than any other single genre of fiction. Doesn't sound like much? Think about this: According to a report by *Publishers Weekly*, Nora Roberts has sold over 200 million copies of her books in print; "an average of eighteen of her books have been sold every minute over the last twenty-one years." What is even more interesting is that in 1993, an article in *Newsweek* magazine stated that mass-market or rack-size paperback sales were over 2.9 billion dollars that year. Even then, romance sales accounted for 53 percent of all paperback sales. Thus, in the past decade there has been a decline in paperback sales. Where has all the romance gone, you ask?

Over the past seven or eight years, romance authors have invaded the hard-cover market with a vengeance. It is common to read the best-seller lists and find Nora Roberts, Amy Tan, Judith McNaught, Danielle Steele, and Jayne Anne Krentz on a weekly basis. Every year, more established romance authors break into hardcover.

Nicholas Sparks is one of a few male romance or "love story" authors who has made a big splash on the *New York Times* best-seller lists, with *Message in a Bottle*, *A Walk to Remember*, and *The Notebook*. His titles sell in the hundreds of thousands in hardcover before they are ever reissued in mass-market paperback.

Just recently, I have discovered, as have publishers, that the "trade paperback" market, the larger-sized, glossy-cover book, is strengthening with the very solid "baby boomer" and even older readers. The surprise has been that the younger, "twenty-something" female reader, who cannot necessarily afford a hardcover book, is seeking romances in this format. To her, a "trade paperback" is a "real book." This new reader mentality is a big shift from the past twenty years in romance publishing.

When I began my publishing career in the late seventies, a few publishers who held an especially loved author at abeyance from her public, usually for a two-year period to build up "buyer frenzy," dominated the trade paperback romance. The publishing career strategy behind Kathleen Woodiwiss' success is proof of this. She and a few other historical romance authors, such as Beatrice Small, cast their magical moneymaking parasols over this format, and for nearly twenty years, few other authors dared enter their private territory.

Then, ten years ago, a publishing phenomenon exploded which influenced a coming generation of potential romance readers. Trade paperbacks were the chosen format for the *Chicken Soup for the Soul* series. These inspirational stories told in short-story form were printed by HCI (Health Communications Incorporated), and turned trade paperback publishing on its ear. Suddenly, the trade paperback format became popular and widespread. Interestingly, the strongest audience buying these trade paperback books was teenagers and young adults. As these groups have aged, they have evolved into romance readers. They didn't have the money to buy hardcover books, but they were now used to buying "real books," which is what they considered trade paperbacks to be.

Two years ago I wrote a nonfiction book for HCI entitled *Angel Watch*: *Goosebumps, Signs, Dreams and Divine Nudges*. This book was a compilation of stories of angelic intervention in my life, my mother's life, and my grandmother's life. When I went on tour for this book, I was astounded at the number of young women—teens and twenty year olds—who asked me when I was going to publish my next novel. When I told them that *The Christmas Star* would be out for Christmas of 2003 and that it would be in trade paperback, just like the

Angel Watch they were holding, the lights went off in their eyes. I saw genuine excitement.

I had firsthand experience with what the marketing departments of the major publishing houses were saying. The day of the trade paperback was here, in spades.

I heard reactions like, "I love how pretty these books look on my book-shelves." "Oh, I never give my real books away." "My books are keepers." This was a definite change from the "paperback" world I had known.

Having raised a teenager myself, I understand all too well the need for the teen to take a different road than their mother. I could see the superior/differ-ent/egocentric place this new breed of readers was coming from. "I never read paperbacks . . . but my Mom does."

Translation: I don't read your novels.

Those words told me volumes.

In the last eighteen months, the larger, mainstream publishing houses have instituted new imprint lines to address these emerging markets. Suddenly, the romance author has a new audience clamoring for romance in a trade paper-back format. This is great news for both published and unpublished authors, because where there is a new venue for readership, there is a new path for the creative person to travel.

Romance readers are different from other audiences. First and foremost, they are die-hard fans. Once a romance reader, always a romance reader. Per person, they read more and buy more than any other genre of fiction reader. It is not unheard of to have fans who read three to four books a week and who spend upwards of a hundred dollars a month on books. A typical romance reader has one or more years of college education. She is often married in a happy or very happy relationship. She reads for escape. She reads for entertain-ment. She is involved in her community and in her children's lives. Nearly half of the romance audience works at a job or career.

These women are vibrant, intelligent, and involved in their lives. They are not sitting at home eating M&Ms with their faces stuck in a book. She generally does not watch series or network television but she wants that story in full-length movies either, in a theater or on cable television. She buys movie videos and DVDs.

In recent years, romance authors such as Sandra Brown, Tess Gerritsen, Janet Evanovich, and others have "crossed over" and picked up a burgeoning male audience. I've always believed there is a "closet" male romance reader. I haven't decided if they are only reading the bed scenes or if they truly read the entire story, but one thing is for sure: once they are hooked, they are likely to read the same author again and again.

Make no mistake, however; the audience you are writing to is primarily female. She has female issues, concerns, interests, and needs. She has power and intelligence and she likes to have fun. She is somewhere between eighteen and one hundred and eight. Your job as a romance author is to find her and make her fall in love with your writing.

A Romance by Any Other Name Is Still a Romance

The umbrella of romantic fiction today encompasses nearly every existing novel genre. This is a fantastic time in our history for aspiring writers. Romance has long been known as the best place to enter the writing field. Why? Because women buy books. As I stated in the introduction, the audience for all fiction is primarily women. The single best-selling genre is romance.

I know I keep pounding you about the reader and her needs and wants, but after this many years of writing, even my editors have gone on record in print stating that one of my attributes is that

I care, and I truly do deeply care—about what my reader wants and is thinking.

I want to share with you a recent report in *USA Today*. This article was dated December 30, 2003.

Hollywood Comes of Age

The romantic comedy *Something's Gotta Give* is a coming-of-age movie. Instead of tracking adolescents awkwardly groping to maturity, it celebrates fiftysomething Diane Keaton as she explores quirky maturity, fumbling sex and all.

For American society it confirms that we are about to overcome our prejudice against older women.

"However, we are witnessing a formidable force that is pressing for a reassessment, and that is the same baby-boomer women who burned their bras in the 1960s for equality with men.

Baby boomer women have considerable clout both in money and demographics. Women ages forty to fifty nine earn more than $1 trillion and control $2.8 trillion in household income. By 2010 they'll be the largest U.S. age group.

For years, these women have been nudging society to recognize them and the qualities they have to offer. Now they're on a roll.

"Older women have resources they never had before: They're seasoned, they're smarter, they're breaking down stereotypes, and they're unignorable," said Susan Crandell, editor-in-chief of *More* Magazine. Since it was started in 1998 to celebrate the accomplishments of women over forty, this magazine's circulation has tripled to 850,000.

Clearly, coming of age is not just for teenagers anymore.

Romance Genres

At no other time is this information as important to you as when you are choosing the sub-genre of romance that you believe your writing fits most. Today's reading audience is as splintered as the cereal aisle in a grocery store. Remember when you had about a dozen different breakfast cereals from which to choose? Now it takes two sides of an aisle that looks like an airport runway to cater to the multitude of brands and types of cereal.

The same is true in romance.

Go back to the quote from *USA Today*. Note that it said in the year 2010 the forty- to fifty nine-year-old demographic will be the largest single group in the United States.

If it sounds distant to you, believe me, it is already on the radar screen of every publisher. If you sat down to write your book today and it takes you a year to eighteen months to write your book—and on a first effort you should allot that kind of time for quality work—then you would need to allot six months to a year to find an agent. Let's say your agent sold the book quickly, within six months. Then the publisher and your agent haggle over the contract; that is another six months. You now will have spent two-and-a-half years on your project. From there it will take the publisher a minimum of one year to put your book on their "list" or publishing schedule, edit the book, rewrite, order cover art, cover copy, print, bind, and ship the book. You can easily see that there is no better time than right now to start that novel.

With this timetable taken into consideration, that quotation from *USA Today* sounds very pertinent and timely, doesn't it?

You should know that a good portion if not many of our top-selling romance novelists started in a category or a sub-genre before exploding into hardcover bestsellers.

Those sub-genres include:

✤ Contemporary Romance

✤ Regency Romance

✤ Romantic Suspense

✤ Romantic Thriller

✤ Romantic Mystery

✤ Romantic Fantasy

✤ Romantic Action/Adventure

✤ Romantic Comedy/Action/Adventure

✤ Romantic Crime Drama

✤ Romantic Science Fiction

✤ Romantic Time Travel

✤ Romantic Paranormal

✤ Contemporary Romance

✤ Romantic Saga/Family Drama

- ❦ Historical Romance (sub-sub-genres: Westerns, Scottish, etc.)
- ❦ Native-American Romance
- ❦ Afro-American Romance
- ❦ Gothic Romance
- ❦ Erotica
- ❦ Women's Fiction
- ❦ Inspirational/Christian Romance
- ❦ Chick-lit
- ❦ Category Romance

I will give you a brief description of the majority of these sub-genres as well as points to consider in your plot and character development that will help direct your story into a genre that will get your book sold.

Though you are writing romance, publishers today are interested in more than just the love story. To emphasize the importance of the direction your story will take in your choice of a sub-genre, I would like to quote the guidelines from Tor/Forge Books: "Each novel should include at least two main plot elements: one, the romance and the conflict inherent in that; two, another significant conflict. Both story lines should be crucial to the overall novel, and the romantic elements should make up no more than half the entire story."

This kind of plot structure is what takes your novel from a "category" romance to "single-title" or "mainstream" status. When you see those blockbuster bestsellers from brand-name authors, you know they have used this dual conflict story line as their foundation.

Mystery and Suspense

Mystery and suspense romance authors include Tess Gerritsen, Amy Tan, Nora Roberts, Sandra Brown, Iris Johanssen, and Jayne Ann Krentz. The list is endless.

Of all the sub-genres this one is the most likely to cross over to the "mainstream" and pick up a male audience. I read an article in *Romance Writers of America*, a review magazine aspiring romance authors should read, in which Catherine Coulter states that 30 to 40 percent of her audience is male. Catherine is another example of a romance author who has spent twenty years writing and is now considered a mainstream writer.

These sub-genres still have a romance as the central *core* theme of the book; however, the heroine is involved in either solving a mystery or crime in which she is personally involved. As a general rule, if the heroine is the detective, the forensics expert, the investigator, or the cop on the crime scene, these are considered crime/drama/romance, and the author should very seriously consider a series of books using the same main character in each book such as in Janet Evanovich's franchise.

As I was perusing Web sites and magazine articles in which the major publishing houses listed what their editors were actively seeking, romantic mystery and suspense were on the top of their lists. I believe this is true for the obvious reason that there exists a high probability that if the author succeeds in creating great suspense and memorable characters, the male audience will find out about it and purchase the book as well. These days it is not unusual for me to be sitting on an airplane and see a Sandra Brown novel peeking out of the briefcase of the businessman sitting next to me.

Thriller Romances

Thriller romances involve the heroine's life being threatened nearly throughout the entire story. *Sleeping with the Enemy* was just such a film, to give you an example. The plot line starts with the heroine being a victim, then she comes to the resolve of getting away from her attacker, usually a husband or boyfriend, and in the process she meets a man with whom she falls in love or who falls in love with her, and the story climaxes with the heroine extricating herself from the crisis/life-threatening moment to find freedom, peace, and happiness at the conclusion. The tension in a thriller never subsides. This roller coaster is a fast and furious one.

Like double Dutch jump rope, the author must not only skillfully work the courtship between her two protagonists into the murder plot or the suspense, but she must keep the tension of the romance at an equally thrilling pace so that the story does not get bogged down. To do this, I recommend keeping narrative to a minimum and using as much action and dialogue between the main characters and the supporting characters as possible. Because there is always the threat of danger hanging over the heroine, her attention to the hero will feel strained at times. For the story to succeed, the author must use a sharp eye and keen ear when the hero and heroine get together.

It is tempting to throw in cute love scenes or unusual meeting places during a thriller plot, but this kind of writing can clang like funeral bells. Every love scene must be easy and smooth. For example, the hero and heroine might be working to solve a murder together. They could both be detectives. To add some tension, let's have the heroine, Jerri, be over-the-top ambitious, very smart, and yet the job she desires above all is the position of lieutenant held by our hero, Tim.

The obvious place for them to bark dialogue to each other in the beginning of the story would be the station house or at work. This is too stale for our hero and heroine.

Again, for interest we would switch gender clichés and have Tim hang out at a vegetarian food store. Let Jerri be the meat-and-potatoes kind of person. Note that we are constantly creating opposites for that clash of magnetism that will drive them to the one place your reader wants to find them. In bed. Then to the altar.

In the beginning of the story we would let Jerri be the aggressor in the relationship, because she wants Tim's job. However, once we have Tim starting to like Jerri's spunk, determination, and her very logical brain she uses at all times, Tim must do the pursuing. In a romance, no matter what the sub-genre is, the man must be the one who initiates the romantic action and ultimately, he must end it, usually with a proposal or commitment of some type. If these elements are not evident, then you are not writing good romance.

In thriller romance, the dialogue needs to be precise, sharp, even clipped and often bitingly caustic and humorous, but the intention of the protagonists must be heartfelt and truthful. This is one genre in which you would never overstate passion. Leave the flowery adjectives for your next historical Regency Romance. You would want to use a light touch when it comes to the romance. You can still use the heroine's thoughts to reveal her emotions, but again, tread softly.

The thriller reader wants something so fast paced that flipping her pages would cause a G-force wind.

The above genres sell well to lines like Harlequin Intrigue, Mills and Boon Medical, Simon and Schuster/Pocket Books, and almost all the big publishers.

In writing circles you will hear "mainstream romance" thrown around with adoration as if it is the ultimate goal. Mainstream romance is defined generally, though each publishing house will give you parameters that define their specific needs, as a story that appeals to both women and men in which there is a romance or relationship but the "action" of the story encompasses more plot than what is determined within the confines of the romance. To appeal to this mainstream audience of males and females, the suspense, mystery, thriller, and crime drama format is most broadly accepted at this time.

Fantasy Romance

In order to prognosticate the future, take a look at what the current bestsellers are in categories other than romance. Look at popular movies and television shows. The single most powerful impact on publishing in the past fifty years is the *Harry Potter* series of books. The economic impact has never been felt to this degree, ever.

The sub-genre here is fantasy.

Fantasy romance has been coming on strong for years and it is picking up. This genre includes fairies, elves, dragons, vampires, werewolves, other dimensional worlds, parallel planes of existence as you would see in *The Matrix*, and even comic book–type heroes and heroines. *Xena* is fantasy. *Lara Croft: Tomb Raider* is action/adventure, even though the Lara Croft character is based on a video-game heroine. *Lord of the Rings* is fantasy. *Pirates of the Caribbean* is supernatural/action/adventure.

I saw a very in-depth interview with Peter Jackson, the writer, director, and producer of *The Lord of the Rings*, and I was struck by an explanation he gave when discussing the writing aspect of this enormous undertaking. He stated that when adapting the Hobbit's tale to his modern-day audience, he kept the idea of Frodo bearing the gold ring to the volcano and throwing it in and "threw out all the rest." He went on to say that creating the "love story" between the elf princess (Liv Tyler) and the king (Viggo Mortensen) was the grounding element for the rest of plotting.

There is fantasy swirling around these characters, but it was the love story that kept the story focused.

There is no question about it; of all the sub-genres, fantasy romance truly allows the author's mind the broadest canvas. You must create whole new worlds, even a new language and vocabulary, as well as explain myths and legends, whether fact-based or ones you invent.

For years, publishing has discouraged writers from venturing into fantasy. The general thought has been that fantasy does not sell. Aren't we glad that J. K. Rowling did not ever hear that piece of advice?

Write what's in your heart. You'll never go wrong.

Paranormal, Time Travel, and Science Fiction

Paranormal, time travel, and science fiction are usually lumped into the same genre, but they are as different as night and day.

Jude Devereaux made the biggest splash of her life with *Knight in Shining Armor*, a time travel book. Her success twenty years ago probably spawned every imitator. I think I've read the book more than a few times. Barbara Bretton is known for her time travel romances. It's a fabulous genre to play in. It's taken the film industry a long time to catch on to this fun-filled romance genre, but it did happen in 2002 when *Kate and Leopold* was released, starring Hugh Jackman and Meg Ryan.

Every year Harlequin Publishing sends to its authors its yearly "Romance Report." This glossy marketing survey gives great insight into the mind of the romance reader. Each year the interviewees are asked to rate their favorite films. Since its release in the mid-eighties, *Ghost* has been a perennial favorite. For 2003, it was listed as number one.

Ghost is what paranormal romances should be, even when you are not blessed with the wacky humor of the role played by Whoopi Goldberg. Paranormal romances not only include love stories involving one or more persons who have departed, but can also include, but are not limited to, dream sequences in which the hero or heroine speaks to the departed lover or interacts with the departed lover. *The Ghost and Mrs. Muir* and one of my favorites, *Jenny*, with Jennifer Jones and Joseph Cottone, also are good examples of paranormal romance.

Jenny is the kind of hauntingly memorable story about a man who meets a very young girl in the park one day. He sees her from time to time and as the meetings occur more often, he notices that she has a crush on him. Then the girl appears to be maturing with each visit. She tells him she lives on the rocky coast near a lighthouse. Fascinated, he goes to visit her home and discovers, now that he's fallen in love with her, that Jenny died ten years previously.

City of Angels is another paranormal romance in which an angel, played by Nicolas Cage, falls in love with Meg Ryan. Stories with heroines falling in love with angels or the hero falling in love with an angel are not considered fantasy, but paranormal by some publishers. Some publishers consider them to be both fantasy and paranormal. However, a novel could be considered paranormal if the hero and heroine don't possess paranormal abilities, but the story is woven around angels who help them get together and find true love. *Miracle on 34th Street* is actually the romance between Susan's mother and Mr. Galey. The fact that Santa Claus appears to be the real thing by the closing scene in the story makes this story a paranormal romance by our definition.

If you decide to write a paranormal romance, this can also include the gothic romance, or gothic romantic fantasy, such as the Anne Rice books. Heroes and heroines would then include vampires, werewolves, witches, warlocks, psychics, remote-viewers, and any other paranormal sensitivities. (Some publishing houses label these romances as fantasy.)

Kathryn Lynn Davis has used the paranormal historical romance genre in several of her novels and accomplished stunningly incredible writing with her psychic heroines. Her epic, *Too Deep for Tears*, is a great example of psychic heroines. Giving the hero or the heroine mental telepathy, psychic, fortune-telling abilities, ESP, channeling, or any prophetic gift is becoming more popular in fiction. Perhaps it is all part of our own evolution as human beings to use more of our brains, but such stories are the very hottest topic for television series, as well.

Just take a look at cable television shows to see what is going on. *Carnivále, Six Feet Under, Dead Like Me, The Dead Zone,* and *Joan of Arcadia* are pushing the envelope started a few years ago by *Buffy the Vampire Slayer* and *Charmed*.

There is one publisher, ImaJinn Books, which is seeking only vampire, werewolf, shape-shifter, witch, paranormal, and ESP stories, though not straight-up ghost stories at the current time. You can get their guidelines from their Web site, *www.imajinnbooks.com*, and they are one of the few publishers I found who accepts queries by e-mail, at editors@imajinnbooks.com.

You will find once you immerse yourself into the world of romance that most of the "new" and "hot" television show ideas have been around in romance for about . . . twenty to thirty years.

Inspirational, Spiritual, and Christian

In the *TV Guide* article dated January 24, 2004, "TV Goes with God," it was stated that this new "transcendental television" was just part of the cyclical nature of the entertainment business (translate that to publishing as well). However, "Other professional TV watchers believe the new shows reflect the impact of September 11 on the American psyche. The terrorist attacks 'changed a lot of the ways that we thought about ourselves and the purpose of our lives,' says Lynn Shofield Clark, a professor of mass communications at the University of Colorado. 'The U.S. has always been a society that's interested in spiritual responses to social problems, so it makes a lot of sense that we're going to try to figure out how to respond to current dilemmas out of some perspective that looks to God—or at least to the realm beyond.'"[1]

This explosion on television directly reflects what is happening in romance fiction or vice versa.

Nearly every major publishing house has launched a Christian, spiritual, or inspirational imprint over the past few years. Tynedale House Publishers, Inc., and Harlequin's new imprint of October 2003, the Steeple Hill Love Inspired and Steeple Hill Women's Fiction, are evidence of the demand for these inspirational love stories that give hope and renew trust in the power of faith.

Again, from my point of view, this is a direct result of 9/11. Frankly, I believe this trend has been coming on for years. I felt the "shift in the universe" around 1995 when my own writing started changing and taking on a life of its own in a new, more spiritual direction.

As our society becomes more and more technological, more computer and electronic oriented, to where we feel plugged in and, too often, unplugged to

[1]Nollinger, Mark, "TV Goes with God," *TV Guide*, January 24, 2004.

our own realities, we are all searching for some kind of meaning and purpose to our lives.

Obviously, many readers are demanding more insight into the romances they read. They want to come away with something more than a few historical facts, a cute hero and a loveable heroine, and a briefly rewarding tension-filled climax. They want something. That "something" is a deeply felt, long-lasting hope.

It is one thing to write a romance in which the love story provides entertainment. It is another thing for your writing to profoundly affect someone else's life.

As a literary person, all commercial aspects aside, it is your responsibility to offer to the reader some kernel of wisdom, a unique thought process that realigns their thinking in a way that makes them see life in a completely new and unexplored manner.

By the way, the above is the description for an award that's given to journalists and writers. It's the Pulitzer.

To alter the paradigm of the public in either their thoughts or actions is a heroic feat, I'd say.

Inspirational romances as defined by HeartQuest, Tyndale's fiction line, are stories "that portray characters of faith who rely on Christ's strength as they overcome the obstacles toward building a love to last a lifetime."

Steeple Hill states: "We are looking for compelling and thoughtfully developed stories that are promoting family values and high moral standards. These complex stories are character-driven and should provide readers with an uplifting and satisfying ending.

"Although the faith element is central to these stories, the degree of religiousness is not. We would prefer that specific Christian denominations not be named. . . ."

Steeple Hill allows a great range of creativity in that they will accept family dramas, romance, suspense, and romantic suspense.

The obvious pitfall in this kind of sub-genre is to become too preachy. The tendency to quote the Bible or other religious books too often will slow the pace or even become cumbersome to the character development and overpower the story itself by swings into religious tangents that have nothing to do with the plot. If you can circumvent these minefields the chance of getting this sub-genre published in today's social and commercial climate is strong, indeed.

Native-American/Afro-American/Hispanic/Asian Romance

Ethnic romance stories have been on a major rise for over a decade. There are several lines in the major publishing houses that seek out ethnic stories, both contemporary and historical. However, BET Books/Arabesque has one of the best reputations for just such romances. Their four imprints feature predominately African-American characters; their guidelines are quite defined and thought out for their "primarily educated and middle-class audience." For example, Arabesque states that the heroine cannot have any sexual involvement with anyone prior to meeting the hero. The hero can never have had a previous emotional involvement before meeting the heroine. They cannot live together because that "indicates there is little commitment." There can be no profanity.

Sounds like a book I'd like to read.

Historical Romance

You can't guess how many times in the last twenty-five years that I have heard that the historical romance is dead. It will never die. This genre is a personal favorite of mine and I've attacked the joy and pain of it at least half a dozen times. If you are interested in historical romance, don't let anything dissuade you.

In researching the marketplace for you and from all my experience, I can state unequivocally that the Civil War romance most likely won't get read by an editor. You can pick just about any other time period or place and you'll have a shot at selling your novel.

I have a suspicion that each and every one of us who is drawn to Civil War novels wants to grab Scarlett O'Hara by the throat, shake, her, and say, "Snap out of it!" Our egos fool us into believing we could have done it better than Margaret Mitchell, but the fact is, she did it first.

If you see a Civil War romance on the stands, my guess is that it is written by a brand-name author who has prodded and pleaded with her publisher to please, please let her write the book that is inside her, burning to come out. Sometimes, there is a wise editor who agrees.

In the past week, I have seen one publishing house come out with a Civil War romance but it was set in Texas, which makes the book more "western" in theme than the traditional "Civil War" venue.

I can't imagine the romance landscape without *Ashes in the Wind* by Kathleen Woodiwiss. Personally, I'm a sucker for Civil War books. I buy them. I read them. But then, that's me. I'm just a reader, right? What do I know?

Historical romances give the author a chance to visit Scotland during the clan wars of the middle ages, the gilded halls of Versailles during the last days of the monarchy, and the formal, decadent palaces of the Forbidden City in Beijing. Love stories are more romantic in costume.

My favorite time period is the turn of the last century, when one could still ride in a carriage, dine by gaslight, and yet see new motorcars and airplanes being invented, and a new century of promise dawning. I love the juxtaposition of the old and the new and the transition of mankind from one kind of thinking and social structure such as America during the Revolution, and Germany in the last days of Kaiser Wilhelm, or Czarist Russia before the Pogroms and the Revolution.

The pitfall in this genre is to get so involved with the landscape, literally and historically, that you forget this is a story about people.

When I was writing my second historical saga, my editor, Page Cuddy, wrote to me that in my first draft, my fashion designer heroine felt to her like a wooden doll, albeit she walked around in great threads.

That comment stuck with me. Never again would I forget that a romance or any good piece of fiction is about people going through change, and, hopefully, becoming wise.

Keep the focus on your heroine first. Your research should reveal to you not only her manners, but also how she would act and react given the social mores of the time. A young girl in 1700s Spain would not walk out the front door without her "duenna." Chaperones are inherent to historical romance. Half the fun of historical romances is providing humorous ways in which the hero and heroine ditch the parents, guardians, chaperones, nannies, aunts, uncles, and cousins who are all conspiring to keep our love-struck couple apart.

Historical backdrops provide the opportunity for you to manipulate factual events to fit your plotline and your characters' development.

In my book, *Wings of Destiny*, I spanned a one hundred and twenty-four–year timeline. Though I cut through the first sixty years with a machete, the final sixty-four years, in which I built a family dynasty in San Francisco from 1842 to 1906, was tediously erected, using over a decade of historical research and printed data, interviews, and eight physical trips to that city. To say that I fell in love with San Francisco is an understatement.

My original novel was more than twelve hundred pages. I made every mistake a writer could make. I not only forgot my heroine, I buried her under so many subplots and intrigue schemes and machinations, she had to haunt my dreams to make me wake up and see her.

When I finally did, Barbara came alive like no other heroine. I can't even write this simple description of this book without getting goose bumps.

This book was—and is—my *Titanic*.

If you are drawn to historical romance, you must know that this is no small undertaking. It will consume you. It will drive you nuts because you will spend weeks, months, digging through research to find one little kernel of obscure fact that will illuminate your plot like nothing else could. You may find yourself interviewing historians or in my case, survivors of the Great San Francisco Earthquake, who will infuse a haunting voice into your supporting characters that simply could not happen in any other way.

In confidence, I have exchanged reflections with other well-known authors who have confessed that had they known how difficult writing a medieval romance would be, they never would have done it. Thank God they did. As time goes on, not enough accurate, historical data is quoted or used in our books, films, and television shows. To precisely depict what life was like in the Dark Ages, the time of Christ, or even prehistoric times, like the Jean Auel books, is a gift of genius and a blessing of patience to the author who accepts this quest.

Again, to help you with some research, I perused the majority of the large publishers and nearly all of them are still looking for historicals. They can be historical suspense, fantasy, time travel, paranormal, Regency, Gothic, and even inspirational, but that historical element is a very commercial avenue to explore.

A word about Regency Romances. Kensington Publishers at *www.kensingtonbooks.com* has guidelines posted for their Regency line, but what is noteworthy for you is that they will accept unsolicited manuscripts for Regencies. That's an open door for a first-time writer, because it can take months or years to find an agent to take you on.

As you glance through these Web sites, jot down the names of acquiring editors, the lines they deal in, and if they will accept unsolicited manuscripts.

My advice on all romance genres in regard to your submissions is this: write the book. Most publishers will state that they do not require anything more than a query letter or sample chapters; your passport to success is to have the book finished. In those instances when the publisher does not want to see the entire manuscript, and they choose only to look at the first three or four chapters, having the book ready for them to see (should they respond favorably) puts you one notch higher than the next person submitting their query letter and who hasn't had the "heart" to write the book. By having the book written you reveal your commitment.

Publishers are interested in writers who follow through. If you are anything less, they will simply say, "Next!"

TWO

Researching Your Romance Novel

*P*undits have attacked romances as not "real books" or novels for years. I'm not the only romance writer who cringes each time I hear this, because all of us work so darned hard to dispel that image.

To infuse our stories with viability, all of us have come to realize that our research is paramount.

Personally, I love research. I get a kick out of perusing *National Geographic* magazines and finding some obscure gem of information that becomes more than background to my story and evolves into a plot device.

Now that is sheer joy, but that's just me.

Hired Help as Researchers

I've met other writers who hate the research process and hire college students and research assistants to gather information for them. I read an article years ago stating that James Michener had fourteen researchers working for him on one project or another.

Colleges and high schools are a great source for assistants who want to help. Some colleges will give credit to the student for aiding a novelist. To contact them, go through the high school student counselors' offices or through the college administration office. I have an author friend who contacted a university English department and found an assistant who worked with her for years.

Don't overlook volunteer aid from friends or family. For nearly twelve years, my mother, Dorothy Lanigan, conducted all kinds of research for me. She went to libraries and to historical societies for information that helped me tremendously. She is also a member of Questors, who study antiques and the historical fact behind such treasures. Her reports on things like carnival glass and antique rosewood have not so mysteriously found their way into my stories.

Mother says that it gave her something interesting, educational, and fun to do in her later years. I will always be grateful to my mother for her help.

There are also many elderly people who are not physically able to work but who want to be active. Reading is a pastime for them. In smaller communities I have found agencies that help the elderly in assisted living areas find just such a kind of work. It will be an adventure for you and for them should you be inclined to hire these very able citizens to help you with your investigations.

Still, the personal touch is most times the best.

I've met other authors who confess to getting so involved in the research that they never get to the writing.

Once you immerse yourself in your writing you will find the avenue and method that fits you best, but a little tried-and-true input from professional writers can't hurt.

The Internet and Search Engines

Today's number one tool for research is the Internet. Some writers will tell you they don't know how they wrote a story without the Internet. Throughout the rest of this chapter I will tell you exactly what they can't remember.

I use Ask.com more than is legal. There are all kinds of search engines and though Google is a good one for people, Ask.com is best suited for those times when you are right in the middle of a very involved passage, with lots of action going on, and suddenly you need to know the particular name of a firearm the hero is using.

Because Ask.com lets you pose the actual question, I find this to be the most immediate route to the facts.

For broad research when you are first formulating your story, other search engines are terrific. You can read entire magazine articles online and get everything you need.

However, when you are in the middle of your "flow," you do not want to lose momentum by reading long articles. If you are like me, I can't get to the next sentence until my facts are correct. As I've stated, every writer has their way of doing things, and some authors can skim over areas where facts will enhance the "atmosphere" of the story or expand the canvas; I'm just not one of them. It is so exciting to find a tidbit of historical reference that lends itself to further plot development.

Libraries and Librarians as Research Tools

If you don't have easy access to the Internet or worse, once you're online, you discover you've blown six hours sending e-cards and e-mails to friends and have done very little about researching your book, then look no further than your telephone.

In the larger metropolitan areas, the city libraries have a phone assistance network that is invaluable. I have used this service for years. Before the Internet, this was the only kind of instant help there was. Each library has researchers and assistants assigned to specific areas such as social studies, geography, history, English literature, and so on.

These people are incredibly intelligent and helpful and frankly, they are better than any Internet site at getting to the meat of the source. You can ask them a specific question and they will not only find the answer for you, but they will cross-reference for you and pull the books if you need them, and you can either pick them up or, in some cities, pay to have them mailed directly to your home.

I am a very big fan of libraries. Half of my novels would never have come to fruition without the educated and enthusiastic aid of these fine people.

Still, for many authors there is nothing like being in the library itself to bring your story added depth. Especially with historical romances, I have found there are times when sitting in the library on a weekend with notebooks in hand gives me not only what I need for the story, but also some new and very interesting tidbit that gives a fascinating new twist to my story. This is what we all hope will happen. It is when this "twist" occurs that the synchronicity that we discussed in the last chapter comes into play with eerie frequency.

One story will lead you to another research book or article and then another. Perhaps the librarian who is assisting you mentions that she personally experienced exactly the subject you are researching. She gives you an interview on the spot that fills in all the blanks you need. Then you go to your car and the radio is tuned to your favorite talk show. On the show is a national celebrity who is speaking out on your topic. You sit in the car and take more notes. And all of this has happened before you've left the library parking lot!

Because this type of synchronicity has been the bedrock of my writing career, and due to the fact that nearly every published author I've conversed with underscores the very same experience, I wrote a book about it. It's called *Angel Watch: Goosebumps, Signs, Dreams and Divine Nudges*. Every writer will have a different interpretation of what is going on with the artistic brain at junctures like this in their writing process. The point is that it is happening. Your mind is making this happen. Just ask the Carl Jung followers. Ask another author. They will tell you this synchronicity is not your imagination.

Along with Julia Cameron's book, my suggestion is to familiarize you with Carl Jung's work. There are several compilations of his treatises and essays available at online bookstores, brick-and-mortar stores, and, of course, your favorite library.

Live Interviews as Research

I am loathe to list my research tools in descending order because they are all important and I've used all of them at different times and in different ways.

Some authors attack their work as if they were investigative journalists. Kitty Kelly, the noted biographer of Frank Sinatra and many others, delves head first into her interviews when she conducts her research. We can all take lessons from her when it comes to writing contemporary romances. If you have a certain subject you'd like to write about, there are no boundaries when it comes to interviews as long as the subject is willing to talk. Frankly, the vast majority of people welcome your interest. The second you mention that you are a fiction writer it's like the floodgates opening.

In conducting interviews, unless you take great notes or shorthand and unless you will immediately go home and translate your notes, I would advise a tape recorder. These days I have noticed that in my professional press interviews I see journalists making notes on laptops plus recording the interview. They are very judicious about what is being said. This is a sign of the times when so many folks, unfortunately, appear to be lawsuit happy.

In fiction, such lawsuits are not as precarious as in biography. You are not going to quote your source directly nor are you going to footnote the quotation. You are looking for background material, historical facts, and scientific data.

Be as well prepared as you can when you go into an interview. Make an outline or a list of specific questions. Also include several questions that have open ends to which the expert can expound. What I've found so many times is that you interview one expert and then they give you the name of a colleague to interview. These are the layers that help you create a fascinating story.

Let's say you are researching a medical thriller. Taking a cue from best-selling authors in the genre, such as Tess Gerritsen, get those facts down accurately. Your reader must trust you if you want her to buy your next book and the one after that. I believe that authors such as Ms. Gerritsen have success because they are judicious when it comes to creating their background. Short of being a medically trained doctor, as a reader, when I pick up a Gerritsen novel, I know that what I'm reading about medicine is scientifically and medically on target.

I have a brother who is the dean of plastic surgery at a huge university. When I need medical information for a scene, if he doesn't know the answer, he refers me to a colleague of his and I not only get the answer, but I get the entire history of the medicine behind it. Twenty-five years ago, I thought all that information was over the top and a waste of time. Now, twenty-some books later, I've used everything he's ever told me.

As a rule of thumb, for historical romances, it is more difficult to conduct live interviews because most of the subjects are dead. At least that's what I thought when I was writing *A Promise Made*, a "natural disaster" historical romance. It was set in Texas during the late 1800s and ended with the single most devastating natural disaster in American history to date, the Galveston hurricane of 1900. Six thousand people were killed in one afternoon. Six thousand.

I went to Galveston for a week and combed the libraries and newspaper offices there. I found the *original* newspaper clippings reporting the events as they occurred at the time. It was an amazing experience.

It is so easy to use online search engines for this kind of information today, but I have to tell you, holding those news clippings in my hands, going into the archives at the library there, and having the head librarian show me articles that few people have ever seen was magical. Something happened in my soul that day. It was as if I had experienced that hurricane, which actually was a tsunami, a dome of water over the island. I remember sitting in a locked archival room and crying for all those poor people.

During that week there I appeared on a local radio show for a charity. There were several people on the show with me who were involved in the community. While on the show I talked about my experience in the newspaper room and the library. An elderly woman was one of the community workers being interviewed on the show. After the show was over she told me that she had not planned to be on the show that day, as she wasn't feeling well, but something had compelled her to come.

"Catherine, I am a survivor of the Galveston hurricane. I lost my entire family that day. I was six years old and I remember it like it was yesterday."

See what I mean about synchronicity? Of course, I made an appointment with her for an interview. She added a depth to *A Promise Made* that I might never have achieved without her. She died a few years later, but her experiences live on in my book.

There is another reason to be as accurate as you can about the information you are gathering. Many was the time I had gone into an interview with one agenda in mind and when I walked out, my entire plot had taken on a new twist and gone into a far more interesting direction.

Make certain you always get all the contact information you need from your source, and that includes an e-mail address if they have one, so that you can ask more questions later once you are doing the actual writing.

In addition, send a thank-you note to your source, and when the book comes out, please send a signed copy.

Your source may turn out to be one of your largest supporters. He or she will tell friends and family about your book and they will tell their friends. Every editor and publisher will tell you that it is "word of mouth" that sells books.

Newspapers and Magazines as Tools

Whenever you are stuck for an idea for a novel itself, look to the newspaper. It's pretty difficult not to find a half dozen ideas for a novel by simply ripping off today's headline news.

When I first began writing I went to a writer's conference at which Tommy Thompson, the author of *Blood and Money* spoke. He had been a journalist for *Time* magazine for twenty years before writing his first novel. He told the audience that he had read about a murder in Houston, Texas, in which a wealthy, socially prominent Houston physician was indicted for murdering his wife, though no one had been able to determine how he did it.

From the get-go, Tommy was fascinated with the story, unlike others he'd been investigating and covering for twenty years. The part of the story that fascinated him was that the wife's father was a real Texas character. He was even wealthier than the doctor, his daughter was the apple of his eye, and he had threatened to kill the doctor on several occasions in public. Thus, the story took on a second layer.

Tommy explained that he flew to Houston from New York to conduct a couple of interviews. He'd expected the story to be nothing more than his next journalistic entry and then he'd move on.

What happened to him is the same story I've heard from other novelists over the years. He got hooked.

Two interviews led to a dozen, then fifty. He spent the next two years of his life using all his time and money to research this Texas murder. For twenty years prior to this experience, Tommy Thompson had made a living being objective. His work was orderly. His life was orderly. Then, with one story, it was as if every brain cell rotated counterclockwise on its axis. His passion for his subject matter became obsession. He told us his interviews grew to over two hundred.

Since that time, I have spoken with other authors who started out to write a simple romance. Once the research began the author was led down a highway to a new life.

I speak with firsthand knowledge about this because it happened to me. I spent fifteen years on one book, *Wings of Destiny*. The story spanned over two hundred years when I started. At one point the manuscript was over a thousand pages. I wrote other books in between, of course, but I was obsessed. The research I conducted on this novel filled my entire study. The book itself began with my father's near-death experience. How's that for an auspicious beginning?

My father had a heart attack at the Grand Canyon, and in the Flagstaff hospital he was clinically dead for over twenty minutes. That is a long time to be dead and come back. The doctors broke all of his ribs and his sternum trying to revive him. Finally, they did.

My sister and I flew through a lightning storm in a little "puddle jumper" plane at midnight to get to Flagstaff from Phoenix, where we had met at the airport, she flying in from Chicago and me flying in from Houston. When we got to the hospital, my father addressed me first and told me that he'd seen a "being of light" while he was dead. This being told him that I was going to write a book that would change the way I wrote forever.

Since I had already written over a half dozen novels by this time, writing a book didn't seem quite such an unusual task whether, given by an angel or not. Still, the story sounds fantastic even now.

The next day my sister and I were at the Grand Canyon watching the sunrise. At lunch I glanced out at the canyon and in the next twenty or so minutes, a new novel in its entirety was revealed to me as if the script had been written by heaven.

My sister has been through this process with me before (though never to this magnitude) so as I related a bit of the story, she egged me on, asking the same question, "And then what happens, Cath?"

Little did I know back in 1987 that I would make eight trips to San Francisco to research the Hearst newspaper archives about not only the founding of that city but the earthquake as well. I never dreamed that I would interview people who had survived the great earthquake of 1906 and that years later I would find a publisher who understood the spiritual and visionary aspects of this kind of romance like HCI.

Again, it was newspapers that provided the research necessary for the novel.

Source material magazine articles provide story background, fact, and data much like newspapers but in greater depth. The newspapers will briefly cover a story, but if you are writing a medical thriller romance, you might want to subscribe to the *New England Journal of Medicine* for news about breakthrough medications or to *Psychology Today* to help you understand the human psyche to create more well-rounded and interesting characters.

To keep your finger on the pulse of this month's trends and to give contemporary flair to your characters, popular periodicals such as *People* magazine, *Town and Country, Lucky, O, Business Week*, and *Newsweek* will illustrate all the phases of contemporary American life that you may or may not be experiencing.

Need some room décor? *Architectural Digest* and the Pottery Barn catalogs will do quite nicely. I like *Veranda*, and to keep me up on fashion, some of the foreign publications, like *Bazaar England, Paris Vogue, Elle Paris*, or *Marie Claire* are a lot more fun than the domestic publications, though I'm a steady consumer of those, as well.

Try frequenting newsstands that have more than just the traditional magazine titles you see in airports. Check out some of the Hispanic magazines. You don't have to read the copy; that's why they have so many photographs.

Also, I can't tell you how many sports, hobbies, and automobile magazines I've bought over the years to get inside the male head. I love those fishing magazines just for the photography. *Car and Driver* helped me buy my newest convertible. I confess to wanting to buy those bodybuilder magazines but they make me too depressed about the extra fifty sit-ups I should have done today but instead I wanted to write.

After all this discussion about research, the most important thing to remember is to have fun. The enjoyment of writing is the experience. If you don't throw yourself into the process, you will never persevere to the last page.

THREE

The Makeup of the Romantic Hero

*I*f you want to make your leading man a real hero, you have to make readers care about him. This is the single most important element in creating a hero.

This is an often-repeated phrase in publishing. The problem is that when you ask an editor to translate that comment into the "how" of creating the hero, most times you'll get a shrug of the shoulders. The answers are more evasive than a Washington politician.

Intrinsic to the romantic hero, apart from the superhero of a fantasy or action/adventure novel, is that the romantic hero's interior and exterior epiphany is tied to his romantic relationship with the heroine.

Think Heathcliffe in *Wuthering Heights* or Tom Hanks's character in *Sleepless in Seattle*. It is not enough that a hero is charming as he moves through the plot—he must be three-dimensional, as well. There has to be some psychological or emotional reversal in his psyche that gives your hero true depth of character. Through the course of the action of the plot and the reversal of the hero's fortune, circumstances, or even his health, your character must grow internally. That is, something dramatic must change within his mind, heart, or soul so that the plot—which, up until the moment of the hero's epiphany, was going in one direction—is permanently altered and begins moving in a different, more satisfying direction.

Think back to the heroes of Greek literature. These heroes were simply ordinary people—with nothing more than human characteristics—facing extraordinary circumstances. It is how the hero deals with his challenge that tests his courage.

The inner psychological alteration from an ordinary person to an extraordinary human being is the *inner* change that must occur in your character for him to become a hero. This transformation doesn't come easily; it takes courage and opportunity to change.

Euripides and Homer fashioned their heroes with serious flaws, an Achilles heel, if you will. But if we look deeper we find that the Greeks believed that a person's greatest strength was born from the flaw that caused him the most consternation.

When fashioning your hero, look to your own inner demons to find fodder for building your Rhett Butler. Perhaps you didn't receive enough attention when you were a child. Do you have an abandonment issue? Do you feel you never got or get enough respect? Perhaps you are very angry about verbal, sexual, or physical abuse either from a parent, teacher, friends, or playmates. Did any of these mold you into the person you are?

Certainly they did.

In the past, interviewers, critics, and fans have all told me that I write "like a man." When I wrote *Sins of Omission*, which spanned thirty years and several continents, I had an interviewer from Sydney, Australia, call me. When I answered the phone he said, "I want to talk to the real Catherine Lanigan. You know, the one who is a man." I tried to convince him that I was myself. He absolutely wouldn't believe me. He said, "There is no way that you could have written Jack Colton in *Romancing the Stone* and now Karl Heilmann and Grant Morgan in *Sins of Omission*. No woman can think this much like a man."

The answer was simple. I write men as human beings. I write women as human beings. I don't try to think more male or think more female for my characters. People are people. We are all one. We all hurt, bleed, cry, laugh, and if we are lucky, we have moments, fleeting, but moments of joy in our lives.

The Greeks knew this. Heroes have flaws. The flaws come from their childhood pains, losses, and lack of fulfillment.

If your contemporary hero is going to save the day for the heroine—or for half the civilized world, depending on where and when your book is set—he must have the attributes at the beginning of the story that will allow him to grow to that heroic end.

The romantic hero is differentiated from other heroes in fiction by virtue of the fact that he must evolve from self-centeredness or a closed heart to loving fully with all his heart. He must commit.

The Principal Traits of a Romantic Hero

"That which makes him great brings him down." Aristotle said this thousands of years ago and it has remained to this day the foundation of every great hero in literature. Your hero's strengths will be the qualities that make your reader fall in love with him. However, in order for conflict in the romance to exist, the hero must be flawed; otherwise, there is no character growth whatsoever and there is no story. The hero must change and evolve into a better person through his relationship with the heroine.

Moving your character through only the plot and the external action of the story makes for a shallow and boring story. Once you delve into the psychological and emotional journey of the hero, you have now added new depth to the story, making your character three-dimensional. Especially in romance, and more so than in a crime drama or mystery, it is this internal journey that makes romances the unique form of literature that they are.

Your hero's transformation throughout the story is one of, if not the key, elements that contributes to a haunting story. To create a memorable hero who will stand the test of time and be remembered long after your book leaves the book-stands, there are several characteristics that you must address.

Below are some prime examples of what we are discussing here.

Compassion

It is impossible for the hero to be the hero without compassion. Without compassion for others who do not have his advantages or talents, the hero would be a cold fish or possibly a psychopath.

Our hero should have heart. He should care. Give him a dog, a cat, or a very spiritual relationship with his horse, but show, don't tell, how open his heart can be if only the right woman were to come along.

You can show in action and dialogue that the hero likes children. No heroine is going to want a man who dislikes children. It is human nature for women to want a man to become a good father to her children. Make certain that your hero has the compassion to care for an infant, play softball with his daughter, and teach his son to drive.

Unless the hero's mother is the villain, he should love his mother. Even if she is the witch from hell, he should still be courteous and polite toward her, even if he wants nothing to do with her.

Compassion fully realized is love.

Strength

The hero must be strong in his ideals, values, and characteristics. From the onset of the story, the reader must see the *potential* for heroic action from the hero. Even if he doesn't save the heroine physically from a burning mansion, he should at least have the potential to do so. Thus, he would be courageous, not foolishly fearless. He would know that he is risking his life, yet he would do it.

If the hero is a lawyer, judge, or legal advocate of some kind, then the hero needs to possess discernment, judgment, and commitment to his ideals.

If the hero is a businessman, he will always be fair-minded. The plot will turn when the hero is confronted with a contract, opportunity, or deal that would compromise his goal of being fair. Give the hero a difficult decision. On the one hand, he helps his company, but by taking the deal, he defaults on a particular promise or side deal he's made with the heroine. Thus, when he makes the wrong choice, he must see the error of his decision and then choose love over money.

There are some heroes whose strength is their physical might. Hercules is an archetype that still shows up in romantic fiction today. There are some stories, not just historicals, in which having a hero who can physically come to the rescue is paramount.

Firefighters, policemen, and soldiers are all examples of this kind of hero. All are very popular with today's readers.

Intelligence

Even if the hero has little education, he needs to be intelligent. He should be able to logic out most situations and prove in action that he has thought through his actions. He can have a Harvard education, but if he doesn't have common sense, your hero will not win the respect of the reader.

Your hero also needs to be smart. Smart is different than intelligent. When he runs up against the bad guys, he should be able to discern good from evil.

The hero should be a good "people reader." If the heroine is naïve and trusts too much, make the hero the one who sees through everyone else's lies.

The hero can never be a dummy. Period.

Kindness

The hero should be kind to all people, rich, poor, friend, or acquaintance. The only person to whom he would not show kindness or fairness is the villain.

The hero shouldn't be a pansy or show weakness. Remember the old saying, "Don't mistake kindness for weakness"? This can even be the theme of your book. In the beginning of the novel, the hero can appear to turn the other cheek or be overly kind, but the day must come when he opens his mouth and stands up for what he believes in.

Loyalty

The hero should be loyal to the heroine. He can fight with her, but when put in a compromising situation, he will always choose to support her. The hero should demand loyalty from his friends.

Manners. Complimentary.

The hero is never a slob in his dress or manners. Even when funny or eccentric, he still will be careful about his personal hygiene and he will conduct himself with good manners in all situations.

The hero is never rude to anyone. This is important to understand in dialogue.

When confronted with the villain, the hero will fight both with words and physical action for what he wants. He can be firm and get his point across, but save the swear words for the bad guys.

Classic Romantic Heroes (Time-Tested and Reader-Approved)

Rhett Butler is undoubtedly one of the best-loved romantic heroes in fiction. He was handsome, intelligent, courageous, daring, dangerous, and incredibly in love with Scarlett. We love him because despite his introductory description and depiction as a "playboy," when the South was truly in trouble, he joined the Army to fight for Scarlett, her family, and her land.

Rhett had no talisman in his life, no crusade before there was Scarlett. As long as he could keep on being a blockade-runner and making money off both sides, he was happy.

He would have done—and did do—everything for Scarlett that was possible until she turned him away one too many times. He understood our heroine like no other person on earth. When she defied convention he was right there behind her to cheer her on, yet he supported her love for her family, from Aunt Pitty Pat down to her sisters.

In addition, he cherished Melanie and adored her strength, and respected her in a way that Scarlett could never understand. In his relationship with Melanie, Rhett became the big brother/best friend image many romance readers want to see in their heroes.

Oliver Barrett in *Love Story*, written by Erich Segal, is a good example of a time-tested contemporary hero. Throughout the entire story we know that Oliver loves Jenny. He defies his family to be with her. He gives up his inheritance to be with her. But even Oliver does not know how deep his love is until she is dying. His sorrow is the cry of immeasurable grief that haunts readers even to this day.

Tips and Tricks for Creating the Hero

Taking into consideration all of the characteristics we have listed for you above, you are on your way to creating a perfect hero. You will also need to give him a fresh voice. To create believable dialogue for your hero try watching romance movies from the last ten years or so. If you use old Cary Grant movies, the dialogue can be too stilted.

If you have a favorite author, there is no harm in reading her books and taking sentiments from a collection of heroes. You can't steal someone else's lines of dialogue, but let's face it—"I love you" is fairly universal.

Listed below are specific tips on how to define your hero even more.

1. **Your hero's strength must be identified at the beginning of the book**. If he is the kind of person who is aloof, holds back, or stresses constantly, he "doesn't want to be involved," then he will plunge into saving the day. Think Bruce Willis in *Die Hard*.

    If he is curious by nature, he will investigate your mystery or crime drama romance. He will also interrogate the heroine to find out what makes her tick.

    If he's reckless, he will rush in to save the heroine without thinking, his courage always at the forefront.

2. **Readers like contemporary heroes to be financially successful.** If the hero is ambitious, then he will always be looking to make himself more successful, which then sets up the ethical dilemmas of betraying the heroine for his own selfish means.

In *The American President*, the Michael Douglas character must make the ethical choice of sending his gun-control bill to the House of Representatives or choosing to support the Annette Bening character with her fossil-fuel bill. For political reasons (i.e., doing what is necessary for his re-election campaign), he chooses not to support his girlfriend's fossil-fuel bill, which he had promised he would support. He loses the girl . . . until he realizes that he was so busy doing his job that he forgot to do his job. The hero redeems himself. He chooses to stand by the promise he made to his girlfriend and to put his self-serving re-election campaign aside. He becomes the kind of man we all hope is leading our country, our people, and our lives. The hero's strength then comes from the hero's flaw and this flaw is what defines the plot of the book. Your novel is always about the hero's journey through life.

3. **Your hero shouldn't have to share the stage.** In romance, though the heroine is usually considered the central character, in no way should the hero play second fiddle. Most romances are half in the head of the hero and half in the head of the heroine.

4. **A real hero has to face his demons.** Whether contemporary or historical, the romantic hero's dilemma must always be his inability or his unwillingness for some reason, past or present, to give his heart to a woman.

Second to using childhood trauma as the hero's character flaw is the ex-girlfriend's or ex-wife's betrayal.

The hottest new romance genre in the marketplace is called "chick-lit." This new genre has redefined the contemporary romance. Every publishing house has a "chick-lit" line these days. When you look at the best-seller lists, the ones soaring to the top are stories patterned after the inventor of the series and her book: Helen Fielding's now classic *Bridget Jones's Diary*.

Time will tell how long this new slant on romance will continue, but from all indications, these stories of young career women—not necessarily the most beautiful girls on the block, but women who are more interested in their love affairs than they are in their jobs—is clearly, concretely here to stay.

The idea of the ex-wife's betrayal is the core plotline in *Bridget Jones's Diary*. This plot is set around Mark Darcy and Daniel Cleaver having been roommates in college and fast friends for quite some time after graduation. Daniel was even best man at Mark's wedding. Daniel then had an affair with Mark's wife, which created the huge friction between the two men before Bridget ever came into the picture. This fact, however, is not revealed until the very last scene of the book.

Mark is reserved to the point of being very uptight, and he is quite put off by Bridget's behavior, smoking, drinking, and saying nearly everything without thinking things through, and yet she mirrors for him all the fun he is missing in his own life because he is still immersed in his past betrayal. Mark has not yet used his inner strength to let go of his pain.

Mark Darcy's Achilles' heel is that he once loved so strongly that he took the risk and married a woman. She betrayed him. He got stung. He refuses to open his heart again.

It's a romance, but it sure sounds like real life to me. And that is yet another key to writing compelling heroes. Make them real.

5. **Even heroes make mistakes**. The fault of humans is that we repeat our human history over and over. We constantly make the same mistakes over and over again. Our countries go to war when we know better. We fight when we should back off, and we back off when we should say what we feel. We seem, as a race, never to evolve. Maybe our high-tech toys improve, but we do not.

Heroes, then, are still learning the same lessons and that story will never get old being told. It is by dealing with his own flaws, his own innate humanness, that a leading man becomes a hero.

Back to *Bridget Jones's Diary*. Mark Darcy challenges Daniel to a fistfight, not so much over Bridget, but about their past. Mark's demons have to be laid waste before he can commit to Bridget. By contrast, Daniel hasn't learned a single thing. After the fistfight in the street in which Mark has soundly defeated Daniel, Bridget basically tells Mark to hit the road because she still believes that Mark had taken Daniel's fiancée from him and that Daniel is the wounded bird here.

Mark does not know that she is under this misconception, so he leaves.

When Daniel comes to consciousness, he tells Bridget that he is willing to settle for her. Stunned, Bridget replies that she will not "gamble the rest of her life on being someone's second best." Good answer. What happens when the best comes into Daniel's life? Right.

When all of the misunderstandings have been put to rest, when all of the internal and external conflicts have been resolved, Mark realizes that having a relationship with Bridget is more important to him than clinging to his wounded heart.

Our hero then risks everything, even the possibility that Bridget may not want him. Common sense tells us that if she truly loves him, she would be available to him should he make the move to ask her for her love.

This, then, is the surface plot of the story, but it is the internal action and heroic change going on in Mark that determines a good deal of the action and leads ultimately to the happy ending.

What makes Mark Darcy such a memorable hero is the fact that as fiercely as he clung to his controlled, unemotional, uptight behavior and life prior to meeting Bridget, with just as much power and energy he turns all of that around when he realizes he is in love.

Every human being, male or female, desires unconditional love. There are no rules or restrictions, no barriers on how much love is given. There is no tit for tat. No exchange. It is total love, given with no expectations from the giver.

About midway through the story, Mark tells Bridget he loves her "just as you are"—a key line that alters the entire direction of the plot and signals a turning point for Mark. This new strength gives Mark tremendous power in the story. He now becomes the focal point of the story, where Daniel used to be center stage.

The entire shift in *Bridget Jones's Diary* comes when Mark speaks this particular line. At this juncture, the action of the book also begins to move in a new direction.

Not only are we using the hero's character flaw to change him, but we are also using it to alter the reader's thinking and Bridget's thoughts, and to move the plot in an entirely new direction.

All of this time, the author used Mark's heroic flaw to create story. She has put him in several situations that keep pushing his flaw to the test until he must change. He can't remain the same man that he was before he met Bridget. She is the mirror to his soul. She reveals to him how much of life he is missing by keeping his emotions bottled up, his anger in check, and by not allowing himself to be, frankly, more like Bridget. Even Mark's choice of equally uptight, ambitious Natasha underscores that his core strength is his control.

Mark channels all his energy into his legal work, yet when he goes to bat for a headline case, it is a case in which an English girl is fighting for her Kurdish husband to stay in England. If extradited, the English girl's husband will be executed.

The romance of such a fight by a woman who loves her husband so much that she will plead his case to the highest court in England reveals Mark's *respect* for a loving relationship and the commitment of marriage.

Sidebar: Naming Your Hero

Your hero's name is a very important element in creating the kind of character that will remain in the mists of your reader's memory. Try to imagine Scarlett without Ashley Wilkes or Rhett Butler.

The name should be strong sounding and not complicated.

Sheldon Gadstone does not cause the angels to weep.

Gabe Turner, Kevin Dalt, Grant Morgan, Christopher Mann, Jed Magli, Richard Bartlow, and Jefferson Duke are all names I have given my heroes.

Names proven to be preferred by romance readers are:

Paul, John, Jack, Rafe, Gabe, Jed, Pete, Sam, Ben, Joshua, Justin, Jason, Sean, Michael, Anthony, Derek, Darren, David, Matt, Matthew, Abe, Devlin, William, Mark, and Steve.

All of these names are very familiar. If you get too offbeat with the hero's name, you lose the reader.

A good rule of thumb is to use unusual names for the supporting character, like the hero's best friend or the villain.

Mark's deepest desire is to be loved, but because of his former wife's betrayal, he is afraid.

This fear is at the base of all of Mark's behavior through the first half of the story. Fear of loving and fear of commitment is the cause of most destructive behavior in any relationship.

Think of how fear of loving translates in your own life or those around you, and you will find all the fodder you will ever need to create a memorable hero.

The Physical Makeup of Your Hero

Your romance readership wants the hero to have some muscles. Sound ridiculous? You wouldn't believe how much money publishers and advertisers put into finding the answer to this question.

The results are that the hero doesn't need and isn't expected to be perfect in body or in any other aspect of his character, as we have discussed in this chapter. Some readers state that abdominal muscles or a "six-pack" really turn them on. For others it's pecs, biceps, or forearms. Half your readers want the hero to have a hairy chest and half want a smooth chest.

Whether he is blond, redheaded, or brunette doesn't matter, but tall does.

The old truism of "tall, dark, and handsome" is still the number one favorite physical makeup of a hero.

Interestingly, physical injuries such as a war wound, a limp, or scars from battle or a gangland fight in which he saved his best friend when in high school all add character to a leading man. Don't be afraid to write about a man with a disease, either, though it's a bit harder to write. Frankly, I would think it would be rewarding to show a hero who overcomes a disease and then perhaps becomes a champion for cancer or heart disease.

Remember, too, that no matter how handsome the hero is, he can never be vain or self-centered or overly concerned about his looks. This is not the guy who will want plastic surgery to look better. He will work out, run, and maybe even be a macrobiotic junkie or a "juicer." He takes his health seriously, but not his good looks.

Even if your hero is the president of the United States and the most powerful man in the world, to our heroine and to the reader, deep down, he is the lovable boy next door.

The only cliché to avoid in drawing your hero is that he should not be perfect. Even physically, he can be nearly perfect, but give him a cowlick, for goodness sake. Otherwise, he's just not real to us.

Putting Your Hero to the Test

Once you have created your perfect hero you need to be able to see if he fits the bill.

After you have finished several chapters in the book and you have created, hopefully, a good deal of dialogue between the hero and the heroine, go back and read his words.

Is he kind and courteous when he speaks?

Is he complimentary toward the heroine? Remember, never use swear words or any kind of phraseology that indicates he is putting the heroine down. For example: The hero would never say "ass" or "tits" or possibly even "butt" unless in a playful manner. You would be amazed at how many beginning writers think this is funny.

Condescension from the hero will get your manuscript tossed in the waste can.

When your hero moves into action are his actions positive?

Does he think before he speaks? Is he intelligent? Does he consider other people's feelings before he speaks? Does he listen to the heroine?

When he tells the heroine that he loves her, do the words ring true? Does he only flippantly say "I love you," and that's it? If so, he needs more work.

Nothing gives away the hero's inner psyche like his dialogue.

Put your hero to the test. Let him speak.

FOUR

The Makeup of the Romantic Heroine

As we discussed in the previous chapter, using her strengths to reveal her Achilles' heel will best portray the heroine, just like the hero.

The generous heroine will be the victim of a scam, or others will take advantage of her.

The curious heroine will find herself thrust into harm's way.

The romance heroine is the focus of the novel.

She is the cog of the wheel and all the other elements of the novel radiate out from her. This is true in most novels in which the action takes place around the central character. The only difference in a romance is that this element is so key that you can never deviate from this point. Especially in the sub-genres where it is easy to allow the murder, the investigation, the villain, or even the hero to become the "star" of the story, you must remember to shine the spotlight on the heroine.

The Principal Traits of a Romantic Heroine

If you remember only one thing in a romance it is that the heroine's story here is about her love life.

This is not a story about how she is the architect of a multibillion-dollar corporate merger. It should be the story of how she falls in love with the head of the mergers and acquisitions team from the opposing corporation.

The heroine's personality should be so strong, so individualistic, that she can carry an entire novel. Within her personality you will need to create the kind of woman with whom women from all over the world can identify.

The heroine should be "everywoman." She will have faults and foibles. She will have bad habits that she either has to overcome or is in the process of moving through. She will have the same vulnerabilities that plague a workingwoman in Lyon, France, just as much as they do a housewife in Tokyo. A woman's loves, life, and concerns are universal. That is the reason romances are globally popular.

Let's look at some key characteristics of the romance heroine:

Intelligence

Your heroine needs to be not only logical but also very smart. Her level of education is your choice, just like that of the hero. She should reason out her choices, think things through, and understand that all choices have both pros and cons to the outcome.

She should be inventive in her thinking and know how to get herself out of a precarious situation.

She should be creative in her reasoning more so than any other character in the book, even more so than the hero. She can take advice from her supporters. Many times her supporters (girlfriend, sister, mother, father, etc.) are the megaphones of wisdom, and those words are the ones that change the heroine's point of view and the direction she takes. However, the heroine must be wise enough to heed wise words.

In some instances you will want a teacher, master, or guide to show the heroine the way, and this is the growth process the heroine must make during the novel. As she is going through her "evolution," the reader should *see* and *hear* the heroine's thinking process. This is where her intelligence is revealed.

Intuition

In addition to the intelligence that the hero has, the romance heroine will rely a great deal on her "women's intuition," more so than heroines of straight fiction, murder mysteries, or horror novels.

The intuition factor is deeply understood by your reader. Don't overlook this valuable method of insight. Intuition, or that ability to follow what the heart thinks and needs, is core to the romance novel. The basic plot, as you remember, is the growth of the heroine from not listening to her heart to a point where her heart is open to love. She can't get there without intuition of some kind at some points.

Compassion

Again, just as we discussed with the hero, the heroine also must have a tremendous capacity for compassion. Those stereotypes in romances of the heroine being a governess in the historical to the schoolteacher in a contemporary novel are tried-and-true romantic characters for a reason. Your heroine must be the kind of personality who roots for the underdog.

She will take on causes. She will march in picket lines for what she believes. She will take a stand and she will defend her rights and her right to speak her mind. She will lay down her life for her child, her lover, and her pets, if need be. She will be the kind of nurturing friend we all hope that we are to our friends. She should not be a bleeding heart, but we should *see* her heart.

Courage

There is no question that your heroine should be courageous. This is what makes her a hero. In a romance novel, the courage our heroine finally comes to find within herself is the courage to love.

During the course of the story she can protect her ranch from the evil cattle baron who is trying to drive her off her land, but what really gives her courage will be the instance when she finally realizes that she can't fight her battle alone. When she allows herself to love the town sheriff who wants to help protect her, then she is courageous. She has admitted that she is vulnerable. She has admitted to herself that the feelings she has cannot be repressed or put aside.

If she dares to love, she can get hurt. Really hurt. In the moment of offering love to another human being, we risk rejection. There is no more tragic story than unrequited love. To live through the tragedy, to experience the pain of heartbreak, and then to triumph with a new perspective and a new life that the heroine has created for herself by the end of the story reveals her courage.

Beauty

This attribute has always been vital to the romance heroine. In historical romances, the heroine must possess a more than average degree of attractiveness. She doesn't have to be the most stunning woman in the story. Many times, you want the villainess to be the most beautiful. However, to the hero, our heroine is the most beautiful woman he has ever seen. He can't take his eyes off her. (We will discuss more about beauty later in this chapter.)

Classic Romantic Heroines (Time-Tested and Reader-Approved)

The one element that makes a heroine a classic is *you*. If you fail to inject your spirit and your heart, your heroine will be forgotten. By immersing yourself into your own psyche and scrounging around for all the insecurities and all the strengths that make you who you are, you are on your way to making a classic heroine. (After all, it takes extreme courage to dissect one's soul and then lay it out on paper for the entire world to read. Think about that the next time you think about what makes a heroine.) Courage and independence are the single most important attributes of the romance heroine. The following examples best exemplify the characteristics of the classic romance heroine.

Scarlett O'Hara

There are no two ways about it. Scarlett O'Hara is still the most memorable heroine in romance. Her imprint on the genre is deep and everlasting. Every historical romance written by contemporary authors is simply that author's stab at re-creating Scarlett. And it will never happen.

Scarlett was spoiled, vain, materialistic, selfish, impulsive, and obsessed with the wrong guy. She was also courageous, fearless, intelligent, smart, creative, and willing to trade her life and happiness to save Tara for her family. She did "Lie, cheat, steal, and kill so that neither me nor my family will ever go hungry again."

For that, we will always love her.

In that one passage, Scarlett embodied the ancient instincts of every woman alive. As women, we were born to be mothers and nurture our young. Whether we take up that challenge or decide it is not our destiny's path in this lifetime doesn't matter. Those instincts are there. It is the reason we love our pets, our plants, and our sister's kids.

The truth is every romance reader has deep beliefs. They do know what passion is and it's more than just the love story.

Passion is loving something or someone so much you would die, or come close, for them.

Margaret Mitchell knew this when she created Scarlett. There are many who believe that women write women best, and that is probably true in the overall.

However, it might be fun to take a look at a few very famous male authors.

Hemingway always had trouble with his romantic heroines and was criticized for either making them sound like men wearing skirts or so noninteresting they were cardboard characters.

Sandra Brown wrote a fun, sexy, memorable romance, *Fanta C*, in the late 1980s for the Loveswept line that has remained with readers for a long time. The heroine, Elizabeth, was a bit prim, but she had a shop, which she called Fantasy C. She is a widow of two years, with two children, when she meets her next-door neighbor one day when her cat gets caught in a tree. For weeks, she writes down her fantasies about Thad in her journals. The point is that the main characters, per se, are not as strong as Sandra's later characters, but that book is one that many Sandra Brown readers will never forget. To create such a character and put her in scenes that stay with readers for twenty years is to have succeeded.

Twenty-plus years ago Kathleen Woodiwiss wrote *Shanna*, which still today stands as a classic romance heroine. This classic phenomenal beauty was constructed within the standard romance plot, but she was more headstrong than most heroines of the genre at the time, and her love for the hero was felt so deeply that readers fell in love with Shanna for life.

Ms. Woodiwiss's talent to re-create a past era and infuse that background with living, breathing characters is an art to which all of us aspire.

From Judith McNaught's heroine, Whitney, in *Whitney, My Love* to Bridget Jones, the classic leading ladies will invariably possess all of the characteristics we have listed at the beginning of this chapter. In addition, they always fall in love . . . even if it's on the last page, as did Scarlett O'Hara in *Gone with the Wind*.

Sidebar: Naming Your Heroine

Naming the heroine is always a lot of fun. Many times it's like naming your firstborn child. Some authors take out the Bible and go through the list of names and choose one that appeals to them.

Intuitive authors "listen" for the heroine to speak to her and give her name in a dream. Sometimes, you have the heroine's name first and then you discover her personality.

The heroine's name does not necessarily have to be strong like the hero's name. Nor should it be necessarily short.

Romance monikers are different from straight fiction, and the name of the heroine is a prime example.

Jane, Mary, Anne, and Susie are about as plain as pie. They are often used in romances, it's true. However, giving them all a bit of flair sure does help.

Jayne, Marie, Annette, and Susannah have more distinction. When you have the opportunity to add an ethnic sound to your heroine's name, do it.

Irish names are a staple of both historical and contemporary novels. Colleen, Bridget, Kathleen, Maureen, Meghan, and Kerry are just as apropos today as they were two hundred years ago.

Spanish or Hispanic names are coming on strong and you should be aware of them: Consuella, Maria (always good, and no, it's not boring), Juanita, and Dolores.

Other names with ethnic flavor include: Sophia, Tatiana, Carmelita, Tanya, Angela, Desire, Renee, Andrea, Victoria, and Shanna.

For contemporary novels, unless you are writing chick-lit, keep the heroine's name fairly clean, but spunky.

Tess, Kate, Rose, Jen, Beth, Elizabeth, Lucy, Sally, Stephanie, Julie, Vicki, Roxanne, Connie, Meg, Ali, Amy, and Nancy are all good contemporary female names. You can put them on the judge's bench or in an operating room in an emergency ward. These names instill confidence and trust, yet they are fun and can be romantic.

When thinking of the heroine's name, imagine the hero whispering her name in the night. How does it sound? Is this the girl you want to spend a year of your life discovering and relating onto your empty ream of paper?

Names like Bonnie, Linda Sue, Babs, Rosie, Sherry, Tiffany, Jennifer, Alice, and Heather (use only in historicals) are best used for supporting characters. Many of them have been overused recently.

I'm always surprised by how many Marys there are in romance novels. I would think editors would get really tired of seeing yet another "Mary book." However, there is just something about that name that all languages appear to love equally.

Tip: Try not to invent a name for a straightforward romance. Contrived names are best used in romantic comedy, fantasy, or science fiction-type romances.

Tips and Tricks for Creating the Perfect Heroine

Trick #1. Make your heroine be the kind of woman you would want to become. All of us have insecurities, and so should your heroine. She should be able to find the strength, determination, and discipline to quit smoking, eat properly, never overcharge on her credit card, and finish the report for her boss on time.

On a deeper level, she should find the courage by the time the story ends to honestly look at herself in the mirror and admit her faults. She should not be afraid to tackle her inner demons, including those from a horrific childhood, if that is necessary. She should come to know herself well enough to know why she is afraid to love, commit to, or trust the hero. If he is perfect for her, then why is she holding back?

Trick #2. Make your heroine your best friend. She should be willing to listen to you at any time. She should be compassionate and hopefully wise. The heroine may not be wise at the beginning of the book, but once she has "run the gauntlet" she should walk away with wisdom.

Trick #3. Give your heroine a sense of humor. Leave the belly laugh lines for your heroine's best friend, but the heroine should have some memorable lines of dialogue. Remember, she can be self-deprecating at times and poke fun at her cellulite, but she should only do it twice in the book. On the third comment about the cellulite, the reader is going to be thinking, "Enough already with the orange peel skin!"

Trick #4. The heroine must believe in true love. She can fight it. She can resist it. But she is looking for it; always has, always will.

Trick #5. We should always be rooting for the heroine. If she is perfect at the beginning of the book, there is no story. She should have faults that the reader identifies with and that the heroine overcomes by the last page. The reader should let out a sigh of relief or be in tears when the story ends.

The Physical Makeup of Your Heroine

Even if the heroine is not fabulously beautiful, give her a couple of physical qualities that set her apart from the norm. Mesmerizing eyes, volumes of hair, and a flawless figure are favorites in historicals.

In contemporary novels, you will now find most heroines have pretty faces, but their bodies lack perfection. As do almost all women, the heroine can even complain to herself or to friends that she needs to lose weight, her breasts are too small, she needs a nose job, she hates her freckles, or she should work out more.

When it comes to hair, there's an old saying: "A woman wears her hair for men and her clothes for women." This is true in romance novels.

Great hair is important to the hero. Tip: Most men like long hair. It's sexy to them. They don't care so much if it's blonde, dark, red, or seven shades in between, but a quick guess is it won't be purple or pink. Even if the heroine's hair is short, she should have it styled to flatter her face, and the color should be described in romantic terms, such as "platinum" or "moonbeam silver" rather than "bleached blonde" or "raven" or "midnight" rather than black. "Amber" is a favorite word used to describe a blonde.

The heroine's hair is never thin. She is never balding. She can have a lot of faults, but the hair issue must be one of her attributes.

Because the "eyes are the window of the soul," the heroine's eyes should be incredible. Describe them all you want in any way that you want, but describe them down to the eyelashes.

The description of the eyes is your chance to reveal the heroine's character traits. If her eyes are steady, focused, and never veer, this reveals that she is intent of purpose, honest, straightforward, and probably wouldn't tell a lie even under torture.

If she lowers her eyelids, she is flirtatious, sexy, and interested in the onlooker.

If she constantly looks away from the viewer she is afraid, under stress or duress, or she is in danger.

Note: There are many books on body language. Read at least one to familiarize yourself with what the experts tell us about eye contact and the crossing of arms and legs and body stance during intimate or confrontational situations.

In terms of height, the standards are less strict; though the hero should be tall, the heroine can be any height. I've noticed more contemporary romances seem to have taller heroines in the past few years. I think this is so because there is less stigma these days about the taller woman and the shorter man. The short, tiny cheerleader kind of frame for the heroine was dropped a decade or more ago.

The contemporary heroine can be just about any kind of body shape you want, but the key is that the hero thinks she is sexy.

As all women of all ages do, the heroine should have one outstanding physical attribute. Perhaps she has a tiny waist or long legs. In historicals, she almost always is voluptuous, because this was what a woman's "charms" were, in case you didn't know.

Give her something beautiful about her body that she is proud of. I remember reading a Judith McNaught historical once in which the heroine's alabaster shoulders were her assets. I've never forgotten those rounded, creamy, alabaster shoulders.

If you place your novel in a foreign country, make an effort to understand what is most sensual to the men of that culture. In Brazil, it would be the hips and butt; in Japan, the neck; in China, the feet. In Italy, it would be the hips. Italian men also like women's shoes that make noise, such as mules with no backs that slap the heel when the woman walks.

When creating your heroine you can give her all the attributes you don't have and always wanted. If you are short, make her tall. Then explore what life would be like always finding men who are four inches shorter. Have fun with your heroine. She's your alter ego.

Putting Your Heroine to the Test

Read the heroine's dialogue. If she sounds vapid, give her some brains.

Watch for the constant use of clichés. Many beginning writers tend to use clichés as dialogue.

In contemporary novels, her words should be precise. Let her say what she's thinking.

In historical romances, the heroine can be evasive, because that was usually the norm in society. She can be quite flamboyant in her speech patterns. Also in historicals, you can use brogues and dialects to give a more realistic atmosphere to the setting. However, dialects are not accepted well in contemporary novels. Various speech patterns, such as New York, southern, or British phraseology, are not the same thing as dialects. These are wonderful if you can do it.

If you can coerce a family member to help you, read the heroine's dialogue out loud. This is not only fun, but you will get someone else's input as to how the heroine's words would ring true.

I have helped many people by editing their books, and one of my most common comments in the margin is, "Our heroine would never say this!" The heroine's dialogue must reflect her personality. If the heroine is supposed to be like the Madonna, make sure her words are not out of the mouth of Madonna, the singer, and vice versa.

If your heroine passes the dialogue test, then she has truly come alive. You have succeeded. Pat yourself on the back. (We'll talk more about dialogue in chapter 6.)

❋　　❋　　❋

You'll get your story off to a great start by creating your hero and heroine early. Having visual images of them as you start to shape the other elements of your story will give a framework in which to write. Once you have your main characters you can begin the structure of the story. Remember to keep in mind your characters' strengths and flaws, then devise methods of how to accentuate and address these traits in the action of the story as you move forward.

FIVE

Romance Story Structures and Outlines

*T*he point of this chapter is for you to find a way that suits your personality and work habits when it comes to organizing the structure you want to use for your story.

Most beginning writers would like to think that now that they have a clear idea of who their characters are they should start writing the book. I would caution against that and spend a bit more time to get down on paper some simple parameters for the story.

It is just so darned easy to get offtrack when it comes to plotting the romance that a few basic story structures written down will help you immeasurably in the months to come while you are working through those hundreds of pages you want to write.

Story Structures

When it comes to writing a romance novel, following a structure grid or outline can prove invaluable, especially since publishers have such strict guidelines. Your manuscript must contain something more than boy meets girl, boy loses girl, and boy gets girl back, but it is still the primary structure. Let's take a look at some popular story structures for romance novels:

Primary Story Structure

Basic to the romance is the courtship, which ends in a betrothal. All romances must have this. For a beginning writer, it is far too easy to veer off course, especially once you get mired deep into an intriguing mystery subplot. To keep you focused, we would plot this structure out in the following manner:

The Beginning: The hero and heroine will meet. That's all you need to write for now as far as the plot.

The Middle: The hero and the heroine break up.

The End: The hero and heroine get back together.

Secondary Story Structure

Within the primary story structure, you will now expand your information to include the next five points. This will help you to flesh out the basic romance plotline you must follow, as dictated by the fact that your story is a romance.

Beginning: The beginning of your story will include the following points one through three. The information you provide here should all fit into this first third or, rather, the beginning section of your story. The primary structure of the beginning of a romance is simply that the two protagonists must meet. The secondary structure involves the atmosphere, the locale, and the geography of the story. The secondary structure is where the hero and heroine come alive. Their personalities must be clearly defined, and the raw bones of the plot, thus the "meet," begin to take shape.

1. Basic setup and introductions: Setting, locale, country, city, and year in which the story is set. This is also where you will put any kind of

backstory about the heroine. Include her parents, friends, school, work, or a threatening incident, if it is intrinsic to the story.

2. Once you have the heroine's story down on paper, do the same for the hero.

3. Now it's time to address how the two protagonists first meet. Where? When? Are there any supporting characters involved?

The Middle will consist of point four.

4. How does the couple break up? Include motivations as to why they break up. If you have subplots, write them here. This is just a skeleton right now, but if you can, add as much detail as possible.

The End will consist of point five.

5. Finally, how do they get back together? Most authors have some kind of ending in mind. Even if you don't, do you know if they will marry in the end? Do you want to end it with a proposal? Frankly, for many authors the ending is the illusive butterfly. They have no idea how the story is going to end until the characters end it. However, as a beginning writer, it is best that you push yourself to come up with some kind of plotline that brings them together. This will help you keep focused.

Utilizing the Primary Structure and the Secondary Structure Method allows you to focus your mind on the story you are trying to tell. This type of outlining is a bit more fun to do and stimulates creativity while simultaneously keeping you from going offtrack with useless subplots and out-of-character actions and reactions from the protagonists. Many times the most difficult task of authorship is holding the reins tightly on your own creativity!

Understanding the Three-Act Structure

Some authors find that thinking in the three-act structure helps them keep and stay focused on the action at hand. I couldn't agree more. This structure helps you know where to end your "beginning" and "middle," and what constitutes the "end." Included below are some expansions on the basic structure definitions outlined above to give you an idea of what is included in each act.

Act I

Act I should consist of approximately ten chapters in a one hundred thousand-word or longer romance. In a "category" romance, you might only have five to seven chapters. This would be the first third of the book and the end of the first act if this were a stage play.

Act I introduces your protagonists to your readers, showing aspects of their individual lives, emotions, hopes, etc. Then, once you're sure readers have an accurate picture of who your characters are as individuals, it's time for you to introduce them to one another. In the first Act, their lives won't change very much, but there had better be lots of chemistry between them. In romance it is always best for there to be some kind of "conflict" right from the start. Thus you would create a potential for them to split up AND to commit to each other by the end of the story. Your choice here is whether you want the conflict to be a result of their opposing personalities or from exterior sources such as evil foes/political situations/natural disasters/career dilemmas, etc. Your first Act should hint at the couple's downfall.

Now that you know what Act I entails, let's look at specifics. Dedicate the first two chapters to introducing your heroine and hero to readers. This is where the reader must fall in love with the characters; otherwise they are not going to read any further. There are no hard-and-fast rules about this, except to say that if your romance is going to have a great deal of suspense, mystery, or some other type of thriller element, you might want to begin with the hero first.

Allude to, but don't *show* us all of his/her personality quirks. If he/she is going through a rough time in his/her life, perhaps he/she is at a funeral. If his/her career is a dangerous one, such as law enforcement, the story could open with him/her staring into a gun barrel.

Within the next few chapters:

In the first act we should meet supporting characters, though not delve too much into their characters just yet.

Establish the careers of each main character and all parameters of the sub-genre you want to explore. (If this were an espionage/spy thriller then you would foreshadow danger by the end of the first Act.)

Act II

The second act, or middle part of the story, should encompass anywhere from ten to fifteen chapters. I have noticed in my own novels that if I'm writing thirty chapters, my second acts usually take fifteen chapters to explore.

In the second act, whatever was hinted at or began to tear your heart apart in the first place gets worse. A lot worse. There should be a great deal of action going on in this section as you "throw the kitchen sink" at the couple. At the same time, they should become even more attracted to each other.

In this section you will explore in depth the psychology of your two characters and expose their vulnerabilities and strengths through action scenes and dialogue, either with each other or with the supporting characters.

While it's difficult to do a chapter-by-chapter breakdown for Act II, here are some crucial elements that typically happen within the middle portion of a romance novel:

- ❧ Create tension by leading up to and including the kiss and the first bed scene. If you want a very sexy book, you can have them jumping into bed at every turn, but you must also create the tension of all this; great sex isn't great enough because the hero is not saying anything about marriage or some commitment.

- ❧ Explore motivations of the villain/betraying best friend/ evil force that will contribute to the couple's breakup. Foreshadow pending doom of the turn of events, and the breakup that comes at the end of the second act.

- ❧ Fully explore the supporting cast and their role in advancing the plot and action.

- ❧ Here is where a great deal of romantic ambiance is explored. If the couple is in Paris, give us a detailed tour of the city while the couple is falling in love or running from the French police.

Act III

The last five or so chapters of the book will then be the last third of the outline. In this last third, you will disclose who the villain is, even if it is the hero's abject fear of commitment. This is the point in which both hero and heroine admit their inner demons or they vanquish the evil stepsister, the terrorist who has held the heroine captive, or the business partner scoundrel who has stolen all the hero's money.

Any and all subplots must be resolved by the second to the last or last chapter. (Justice must prevail.)

The hero must declare his love for the heroine.

The heroine must declare her love for the hero.

The couple must commit to each other.

Creating an Outline for Your Novel

When you are first attempting to write a novel, and I mean up until about your sixth or seventh book, you will be self-sabotaging if you don't create an outline first. Using the tools discussed above, let's discuss how to create an outline for your romance novel:

Step 1: Write a Short Synopsis

When a story first hits you, immediately go to the computer and write a synopsis. Most authors write a short synopsis consisting of two to six pages. However, there are many authors who can't stop writing. I'm one of them. My "short" synopses tend to be about thirty-five pages, sometimes more. This will come out in a very long day and probably a night.

The next day, go back and add more scenes to create a richer plot.

Step 2: Create Character Sketches

Next, write the character sketches of the main four or five characters. This will take a week or more. Some of these sketches may be as long as twenty pages each, especially for the hero and heroine.

Step 3: Create Setting Sketches

This is where you finally put a great deal of your research down on paper. Include historical anecdotes you want to use: specifics on a restaurant, wines, or an unusual dish—anything that adds ambiance to the story.

If you can, tear out articles, recipes, interesting room designs, or photographs of cars, horses, boats, and jets, and keep them near the computer. As you outline, which we will discuss in a moment, staple the appropriate article to the back of each chapter's outline that you want to use.

Step 4: Write the Outline

To make this process as simple as possible for you, I would suggest using the following format: Start by giving each chapter its own page. (If you have a great deal of information for chapter 1, use more paper.) Staple those articles about decoration, history, or setting—anything you have found in your research that pertains to this chapter—to the back of the corresponding chapter page. Do this with every chapter you are writing.

Remember, for a large mainstream or historical romance, you will want anywhere from twenty-five to thirty chapters. You could have more but probably not less.

"Category romances" will have fifteen long chapters or twenty short chapters.

Let's take a look at what a sample outline would look like:

Title

ACT I

A. Chapter One

  1. Introduce heroine

    a. Describe physical makeup, age: Jessica was a tall waif of a young woman who had no concept of the impact of her light-haired beauty on the opposite sex.

    b. Describe dwelling: Small apartment, too many plants, a dog, but a control freak. Clean, neat, even has her clothes categorized according to colors in her closet.

    c. Describe her job: Jessica was understandably bored with her job in auto sales, since she constantly outsold every salesman in the dealership month after month.

    d. Describe current dilemma at work: She's being fired. Introduce best friend. Boss. Two male coworkers.

    e. Device to bring the protagonists together: Heroine's car does not run. Must be towed.

B. Chapter Two

Repeat process for hero. Hero meets heroine in this chapter.

  1. Introduce hero. (Repeat steps A through E listed above.)

  2. Hero and heroine meet.

    a. Location of meeting: auto shop.

    b. Hero owns the shop and makes plan to return car to heroine's house the next day.

C. Chapter Three

  1. Hero advises heroine her car is shot. She should buy a new car. This is very ironic to the heroine since she is a car salesperson. This introduces humor.

  2. New twist: Other salesmen have plotted against Jessica and get her fired. This introduces intrigue. Jessica now cannot afford new car.

Outlining Act I

Continue with this process until you lay out the entire Act I. Try to lay out ten chapters for Act I. You won't know what is going to happen in each chapter but as you delve into your research, you will find more interesting plot points. Perhaps the heroine has always wanted to go back to school, and instead of working as a bookkeeper for the hamburger joint she's been working in since high school, she really wants to become a CPA. Your research could reveal how many classes she would need, the cost, and so forth. All that should go into your outline. How is she going to find the money for these classes? Can she apply for a student loan? Will the hero lend it to her?

In the first chapter outline try to show the heroine's characteristics by the way she lives and conducts herself. Don't *tell* us that she is a neatnik. *Show* us by the setup and over-the-top organization of her apartment.

In the outline for the second chapter, be sure to reveal the hero's characteristics by the events you place him in. Even if all you want to show is that the hero is daring, dashing, and a rescuer, then do it in an action-packed manner.

Continue outlining your chapters until you have brought the couple together. The hero and heroine have created an attraction and you have created those elements that may either pull away from the other or fall apart from within themselves, which would cause a breakup or cause external forces to interfere with the couple being together.

This first third of the book or ten chapters will be your Act I.

Outlining Act II

Keep outlining until you've laid out fifteen chapters for Act II. Outline your Act II giving as many details as possible to both plot development and character evolution. I've heard many times from editors that the middle sections of novels written by first-time writers almost always get bogged down.

The solution is to throw more crises at the hero and heroine than perhaps even you had thought possible. If the heroine is not being flogged by life, circumstances, and those around her, the story will plod. This is so true in real life. Just when you think things can't get any worse, they do.

How many times have you heard of a friend or acquaintance or even read in the newspapers about celebrities who suddenly got divorced, lost their job, found they had a terrible illness, or had a close relative die all at the same time or within just a few months?

The law of physics tells us that once a certain energy, negative or positive, is exerted, it attracts like energy to it. Thus, downward spirals of your character's psyche and moods will manifest in outward circumstances. Art imitates life. Make certain you include these points.

For strong measure, write the words "negatives" and "positives," and then list those circumstances to keep you focused. List the incidents that happen to the couple that create their "downward spiral."

Use those events that you *know* about to flesh out your characters. Put those events in your outline to give you guidance.

The middle part of the novel, for me, is the best part. This is where I really get to test the mettle and courage of my hero and heroine. Your story doesn't have to be a thriller to make the scenes thrilling.

Let's say our heroine is a working girl. She's banged her nose against the glass ceiling so many times, she has a nosebleed. In fact, she's never had time for love because she was always working. Then, just when she's given up hope that princes do not exist, she meets Mr. Charming. He falls madly in love with her. His kiss is divine. After a month of dating, he's already talking wedding bells.

She goes into work one morning, and the big boss calls her in and hands her the promotion she's dreamed about for a decade. The problem is that she has to move to Spokane.

How this couple works this out and their reactions to this dilemma are the same things we all face every day.

Outlining Act III

Again, there should be five to seven chapters for Act III. Here you will bring all the story elements, those fabulous threads you've been weaving into one fine fabric. You must interconnect all the elements, the characters, and the plot together to create your happy ending.

If you wind up with any plots, devices, or even characters that do not fit, cut them. Editing yourself in the outline phase of writing is easier than doing it when you have three hundred and fifty pages staring you in the face and your novel is not working

It is not necessary to adhere to a very strict outlining format at all. Just do what feels comfortable for you. As you progress and your creative juices kick in, you'll find yourself writing all kinds of notes and ideas. The point is to get them down on paper. No one is ever going to see your outline. It's there for your eyes only!

Putting It All Together

In each of your chapters, plan to end with a cliffhanger. This is not always possible, especially in the chapter in which the hero proposes, because while your heroine says "yes," you have set up the plot so that readers know something dire is about to happen in the following chapter. Without that lingering tension, your story can sputter to a halt.

Some chapters *need* to end with an intake of breath to give the reader a break. Obviously, the chapter in which your hero finally kisses the heroine, and then either she invites him into her apartment or he says goodnight, is the satisfying "ahhhhhhh" the reader has been frantically anticipating for many pages. I call these chapters the "commercial break" chapters. The reader should feel like going to the pantry, grabbing a chocolate bar, peeling back the wrapper, and then opening the book for the next exciting installment. If you do your work correctly, and end each of the next five or six chapters with a cliffhanger, you've got the reader hooked.

It's often easiest to create these finger-clutching chapter endings by doing your homework ahead of the actual writing. Now that you have your twenty or thirty chapters divided out, refer back to your character study notes.

Each chapter outline should have three main points:

1. The character's development due to the circumstances of the plot. Internal character growth, which affects the plot.

2. The movement of the plot forward, outside the main characters and their internal growth.

3. Some foreshadowing of future outcomes: those of the upcoming chapters and the possible ending.

Subcategories to cover in each chapter would be:

1. Historical references/information/interesting data to describe the background or geographical area/time period

2. Subplots

3. Supporting characters' involvement in the plot

All of the above guidelines answer the question, "What's going on right now on this page?"

Genealogy Grids

It is very important to create a heartfelt heroine or hero, and one of the best ways to do that is to introduce the family. Aunts, uncles, cousins, parents, and siblings give you room to explore your own comedic skills as well as delve into the psyche of the hero or heroine through the eyes and actions of the relatives.

Sidebar: Using Index Cards to Outline

I am including this subject because I have been asked about this system of outlining so many times by aspiring authors.

The three-by-five index-card system offers a very simple and organized approach to outlining. If this system of jotting ideas down and then alphabetizing them to suit your story works for you, then by all means use it.

There is no "system" by which three-by-five cards offer some magical organizational skill other than what is explained above. However, if you wanted to put your Three Act outline on three-by-five cards and file all your ideas on these cards in the three areas, then you would want cards with headings that would at least include:

❧ Characters. Include all the particulars you would have in your character sketches.

❧ Settings. Include a card on each city you are researching. Museums. Restaurants. Cultural events in the locale of your setting.

❧ Plot points

❧ Subplots

❧ Research items: Weaponry. Clothing. Cars. Motorcycles. Airlines. Any and all odd pieces of research information you need.

When I traveled to Los Angeles during the shooting of *Romancing the Stone*, Kathleen Turner asked me this very question:

"Do you use those little index cards, and if you do, what do you do with them? Do you put them around the room?"

Not only did I use those cards, but I also used paper towels, bank deposit slips, and toilet paper—anything that was handy.

Since the invention of Post-It Notes, my study is now a very colorful blizzard of stick-up notes all over the face of the computer, the walls, and windows. For years, I posted my family trees, notes, pertinent *National Geographic* articles, handwritten research notes, and scribbles of ideas on a corkboard near my desk.

Today, I have a huge worktable in my study and I spread everything out on the table in semi-neat piles. I have two file cabinets behind the desk that give me more space to lay out research, my pin-the-tail-on-the-donkey timelines, and favorite Internet download information. It has taken me ten years to break the habit of pinning my research on the curtains and the backs of chairs, and taping things to the walls. (I could never get the tape off the walls properly, so I used this as an excuse to paint the study again until the walls were so thick with paint I was losing valuable square footage.)

In historical romances, you will find the family tree device even more helpful, since meddling cousins—kissing or otherwise—along with all the other pertinent relatives, were usually the majority of social contact that most young ladies would have had a hundred years or more ago.

If you've never seen a family tree, it looks just like . . . a tree. On the right side is the groom's family; on the left side is the bride's family.

Start by placing the bride's name at the left root of the trunk of the tree and the groom's name on the right root of the tree trunk.

Both protagonists have to have parents, right? Give them names. Add a brother or sister and maybe some in-laws. If your mind is in the least creative—and we have to assume it is, otherwise you wouldn't want to write a novel—you will find a number of backstories coming into your consciousness like the Jamestown flood.

Ancient wisdom and some modern DNA research and science tell us that we are all a sum of our ancestors. If this is true, then those backstories about the heroine's mother could be the characteristics that make our heroine strong or fearful or lovable.

The further back you trace the family tree, the more stories you will create and more richness you will bring to the characters.

A number of authors have told me that when they were drawing up those first family trees for their novel, they were actually writing prequels to their story.

Never throw away those family trees. If your book becomes a hit and you've just created the next "Calder Family Tales," then you will want all that research.

As you work on the family tree, at the same time, on separate sheets of paper or on the computer, place each ancestor's name and then begin a character study sheet for each of them. None of this work will be wasted. You don't have to write a short story for each one, but you should have a paragraph explaining who this person was and what influence this person might have had on our heroine or hero.

These grids will serve you more than you can imagine when you are writing larger family sagas or more complex romances.

When she first began writing, Jude Devereaux used to sew doll costumes to resemble the main characters in her novels. I will never forget the article I read about Jude back then. When I met her in person at Judith McNaught's house, I commented on how interesting I found this practice of hers. She told me that having those costumes helped to bring the characters alive for her.

What wonderful advice that was.

Do whatever it takes to help you get into the heads of your hero and heroine. Perhaps you would like to build a little dollhouse to illustrate the setting where your story takes place. If you can put your imagination and your heart into that place, your readers will only benefit.

Timeline Grids

Let's say you absolutely loathe and despise the idea of working with an outline, but your novel is one that is going to span two generations. You know you need to produce at least some kind of skeletal structure.

Let me introduce you to the timeline grid.

When you begin your novel you must decide over what period of time the story takes place. Most thrillers only span twenty-four hours. An historical novel could encompass two hundred years. Romances are obviously all over the place as to length of action, but whether short or long, the timeline is important for pacing.

In the film industry, "having a timeline" usually refers to the plot point device used to create tension, such as: a ticking bomb; the kidnappers' ultimatum of a deadline before someone is murdered; a rescue attempt before the heroine is hanged; and devices of this nature.

When it comes to the writing process, "timeline" refers to the actual length of time of the story. For example, in my novel, *The Christmas Star*, I have a timeline of thirty years. The Christmas Star is an actual celestial event that occurs every thirty years, with a crescent moon appearing in the western sky with Venus hanging off the tip and Mars suspended right beneath it.

In the story, I needed the action to begin basically around the first Christmas star in 1965 and have the happy ending with the return of the same star in 1995.

To create the timeline grid I literally drew a line on a sheet of paper. The beginning point was 1965, when Susie and Tommy met. The next plot point time was March 1966, when Susie realizes she is pregnant, they run away and get married, her parents disown her, and Tommy goes off to Vietnam. The next point on the timeline was September 25, 1966. On that night, Tommy's secret mission goes awry and everyone on his helicopter is killed except Tommy. At the same moment Susie nearly dies in childbirth; their twins are born that night.

The next timeline is six months later when Susie's father reconciles with her and Tommy recovers physically, but not mentally from his wounds and must remain in captivity.

The plot points on the grid then went in five-year increments, showing what was happening in each character's lives at each Christmas until 1995.

Using this very simple outline method, you can lay out the bare bones of plot point turns and some character development and keep the years straight. In a story such as *The Christmas Star*, and many others, it was important to keep the ages of the children straight, along with those of Susie, Tommy, her parents, and Tommy's father, Jed.

I have done timeline grids that look like Pin the Tail on the Donkey. I will take small scraps of paper and write notes on them (yes, this is how bank deposit slips are intended to be used), and tape them to the timeline grid.

This is an elementary-schoolteacher's methodology, but I love it because I can move my notes around, change characters' introductions, and do all kinds of experimenting with my story before ever writing the first page.

There have been times when I've come up with a story, laid out this first of my outline devices, and trashed the story completely. If the story fails this first timeline test, the story is a clunker.

And what is that test?

My interest.

If you start with an idea and it doesn't go anywhere, if there aren't any supporting characters automatically coming into my consciousness, if the heroine tends to be reactionary as opposed to proactive, or if the hero is without strengths or interest to me, you can be well assured that nobody else on the planet will care.

If your story passes this acid timeline test, then you can move on to outlining, your family trees, character sketches, or even go straight to the computer.

❋   ❋   ❋

Every author has her own particular and peculiar method of how to start the process of writing. When you start out to write, you should organize and plan as much as you can to help you know your own characters better. There will come a time in your story when the plot will put you at a crossroads and your heroine will have to open her mouth and say something that will be her "defining moment." To know exactly how she would say, "I can't think about that right now. I'll think about it tomorrow ... at Tara," you will have to have known your heroine down to her DNA.

SIX

The Mechanics
of Writing
a Great Romance

*O*nce the plot is down on paper and the characters are dancing around in your head, it is time to start writing the book. In this chapter we will explore not just grammar and composition, but how one goes about defining your personal style, or "voice."

Choosing the Right Point of View

As a general rule, romances are all written in the third person. The main reason for this is that it allows the author to exploit the "heads" of both the heroine and the hero and, when called for, even the thoughts and ideas of various supporting characters.

If your romance is a mainstream story or a strong sub-genre such as mystery, thriller, or suspense, the story is usually made stronger by visiting the villain in his or her lair and discovering as much as possible about the villain, their plot, and their reasoning. This is accomplished best when the story is written in third person.

That said, in the past six years or so, and with the introduction of the "chick-lit" genre of very popular romance novels, the first-person point of view is gathering a huge head of steam. A few decades ago, bestselling romance novelists steered clear of first person point of view because of its vast limitations. The belief was that this kept the story "small." There was little room for exploration of character development.

The Janet Evanovich series of Stephanie Plum mystery romances is first person and offers a prime example of first-person point of view. *Bridget Jones's Diary* is also first-person point of view.

However, most publishers will state in their guidelines that the point of view for "chick-lit" can be either third person or first person. Thankfully, there is an option, but the majority with the most humor tend to be first person.

The vote is split as to whether for a beginning author this is a good place to start or not. This needs to be a personal decision when you first start the book. It will change the method in which you outline and form your structures because the burden of the storytelling will be on the heroine.

Most editors prefer you start your writing career in the third person.

Plotting Your Romance

Many beginning writers have problems with "What happens next?" As you begin to formulate your plot, there will be times that you just don't know *exactly* how the heroine is going to escape from her captor or find the money to save her house from being foreclosed upon. Sometimes these are just the points that need to come to you during the writing and are best left until you are actually writing.

To help you get to that point, however, you need to formulate as much plot as you possibly can before you start writing.

Beginnings

Again, take out a stack of paper. You'll need a few sheets for your beginning, middle, and end. Staple three or four sheets together for each section. This gets you used to the idea of filling up pages with useful information and with story ideas.

From the very start, plan to open your story with a killer sentence. It is vital that you grab the reader and your editor on the first sentence. Editors, especially, are sensitive to a great beginning. It is not uncommon for an editor to reject a book if she doesn't like the first paragraph.

If your story is a romantic thriller, a killer first sentence is much easier than a straight romance, to a degree.

In my book, *Tender Malice*, my opening sentence was: "Karen faced death with her eyes wide open."

"After today, your life will never be the same." That was the opening sentence for *Wings of Destiny*, a historical romance.

The point here is to be *intriguing*.

Use your first killer/grabber line to be indicative of the plot you are about to unfold.

In *Wings of Destiny*, Jefferson harbored a dark secret from his past that he successfully hid for eighty years. At the beginning of the story, after which follows the flashback to the entire novel, he realizes he must now tell his granddaughter something that may result in the loss of her love and respect. Because she is the only family left to him, the love of his life, and his reason for living, this is the nightmare that has haunted him since he was sixteen.

That's a lot to say in a couple of sparagraphs, but it is vital to create enough tension and tease that you will keep the reader reading.

Beginning Step One

When charting out your plot as you are doing here, write down the main plot of your story. For example:

Main plot: Ali hates Zack at first sight. Zack's boss forces him to work with Ali. Ali must work for Zack and she sabotages everything he does. Zack falls for Ali, she starts to fall for him, but doesn't trust him. Secrets are revealed from Ali's brother. Zack and Ali lose their jobs and form a company together. They commit.

Beginning Step Two

That's the basic plot.

Now we expand.

Zack meets Ali at her brother Drew's New Year's Eve party. Zack has "crashed" the party, walks up to Drew, and punches him in the jaw, knocking him to the floor. Zack accuses Drew of abusing his sister, whom Drew has been dating for the past four months.

Ali listens to Zack's tirade, hauls back, and punches him in the stomach, and then lifts her leg and kickboxes him, sending him to the floor. Ali orders two of Drew's friends to throw Zack out.

In the beginning plotline, you now have Ali hating Zack, defending her brother, and wondering why Zack's sister would be saying such things about her brother.

After this first encounter, plot out two more accidental meetings between Ali and Zack.

Perhaps Ali is interviewing for a new job at an advertising agency and she's going back for the final interview. She's passed the folks at human relations and they all like her. Now she needs to meet the boss, who is, of course, Zack.

He does or does not hire her.

Then, plan another time when they are thrown together. Perhaps she takes the job with Zack's competition. (My choice, because there is a greater chance for more conflict, and you can keep the antagonism between the two going as Ali comes up with a better ad campaign than Zack. Now, Zack would really despise Ali and vice versa.)

This would get you through the first third of the book.

While you are plotting the romance, you need to create sexual tension between Zack and Ali.

It is best to plot out where you want these triggers to be. One will be the minute Ali sees Zack coming into the party. Perhaps he's the best-looking man there. Maybe he's wearing a tux and everyone else is in fun, flashy clothes. Therefore she would notice him.

Perhaps it is the opposite. She is in a stunning gown, coming down from a staircase, when Zack first enters Drew's apartment. He can't take his eyes off her.

Plot a scene in which Zack goes home and can't stop thinking about Ali, even though he's satisfied/not satisfied about getting retribution for his sister.

Plot a scene with Ali and her girlfriend in which Ali confides she hates Zack. She's adamant about what a rat he is. However, this is three days later and her girlfriend is now not buying her story. Why can't Ali stop thinking about him?

Third sexual tension scene: Zack sees Ali coming into his building on the day of her interview. He doesn't know why she is there. He hides behind a marble pillar . . . just to watch her.

Fourth sexual tension scene: Ali walks into Zack's office and her first reaction is that she smiles at him. She's happy to see him. He frowns/smiles back.

Whenever possible, place as many scenes now as you can on your plot plan paper.

Middles

As you move into the middle section of your book you need to start exploring subplot. The subplot here that reflects on the main plot of Zack and Ali getting together is the relationship between Zack's sister and Drew.

This is also the place where you could bring in more office rivalry by having Zack's boss, Bart Mellon, a very greedy, contentious ad agency owner, discover that Zack did not hire Ali when he had the chance. Bart demands that Zack get Ali back or lose his job.

To keep the middle from bogging down or sagging, use action and dialogue.

In the previous section you would have had to spend a lot of time giving background on your characters, location settings, and descriptions of where the characters live.

In the middle, expand these points, but do it in action. Such as:

* Zack has a dog that he takes to the park to walk. It's the same park that Ali jogs around on Saturdays only. Because of her new ad agency job, she's doing a lot of late-night work. Her early-morning Saturday runs have been altered now from six in the morning to eight.

* Zack always walks Beau at eight. Now they run into each other.

* Create action and dialogue between Ali and her brother. Add their mother with a family Sunday dinner.

* Create dialogue scenes between Ali and Zack the day they are both going in to pitch a new car company as they bid for the same job.

* Create another action scene in a restaurant where they are both dating other people and see each other that night.

* Middles can be fun when you make your scenes inventive. During this middle section you must create more antagonism between the pair while at the same time creating or setting up the time when they will finally bond. The obvious choice here is that the car company account is a multimillion-dollar account. Both agencies want this account.

* Zack is supposed to be trying to win Ali over to his company. He has to figure out a way to entice her to

join forces with him to win this account. It would be better than if XYZ ad agency gets the job, right?

* Now they have to work together. He gains respect for her because he sees firsthand that she is really good. She sees that he's not such a hothead after all.

The middle, then, expands the beginning and sets up for the ending.

Endings

The ending is where you finally weave your tapestry of love together to create the happy ending. To plot this you must go through your story with a fine-tooth comb.

On paper you must list:

* The subplots you have used to create all conflict.

* All characters that you can use in any way to help bring the couple together.

* List the single alteration in each protagonist's character that would turn their heart around.

Take the subplots and flip them one hundred and eighty degrees. In our story scenario above, Ali disliked Zack because he beat up her brother. Zack disliked Drew and by virtue of Drew, Ali, because his sister had told him that Drew was being abusive to her.

* Flip the story. Turn the negative plot or subplot to a positive. Let's say that it was Zack's sister who is the whacko. Drew discovered after four months of dating her that she's a nutcase and broke up with her.

* Zack has misunderstood all of this.

* Therefore, in the end plot point turns, you should have a scene in which Zack discovers the truth from his sister in a poignant "confession" scene. She doesn't have to be evil, but maybe she's a bit spoiled. Maybe she really wanted Drew but didn't know how to keep him after the breakup so she was lashing out and told this lie. She needed the attention from Zack. There are a million reasons you can use.

* This still does not get Zack back in good graces with Ali.

* The heroine's self-discovery/The hero's self-discovery.

  * This plot point element must always come in the last few chapters or in the third act. It is the moment of revelation when the hero realizes he is in love with the heroine, but he doesn't know how to get her back.

* Revelations. In addition to reversal of any subplot changes, this is the point when other characters also should come together. In this story it is up to you if you would want Ali and Zack to both quit their jobs because they don't like how their bosses are handling their accounts. Perhaps they won the bid, but it has been revealed to them that their bosses are both out to screw our hero and heroine out of their commissions.

* This would be the time that the story line involving Drew and Zack's sister can find some kind of conclusion. Do they start all over, or just become friends? In a romance you MUST give them some kind of satisfying closure. Don't leave them hanging out there.

* Once Ali and Zack lose their jobs, they are thrown together again in a scene on a bus or the train, or they run into each other in the park again. Their defenses are down. Ali is finally willing to listen to Zack as he opens up and reveals his feelings.

* The "tag" or "tie-up" would be that they decide to form their own ad agency together.

Once you plot out these elements you have enough of a framework from which to sketch your characters and really flesh out the story to its magnificent potential.

Using Dialogue and Action in a Romance Novel

Action and dialogue are the bones of your story. They are the poetry. Screenplays are all action and dialogue, with action scenes described in the barest of detail. If an entire film can be made from action and dialogue, you realize how vastly important they are to the novel format.

Your reader will fall in love with your characters *if* she cares about them. Your job as the author is to evoke that emotion by portraying the heroine as vividly as possible. Realistic dialogue can help you achieve this.

Your heroine's dialogue is one of the single greatest components to making her unique—it's her way of stating herself in her own voice. If you let your action overshadow your dialogue, however, you're limiting your character's chances to show readers who she really is.

My first book, *Bound by Love*, was originally nearly eight hundred pages. I had to cut it almost in half before Avon would print it. In the original version, I had four sisters, and Elise Kendall was the eldest. I had a whole lot of interaction with these sisters that had nothing to do with the plot. My first directive from my editor was to eliminate the three sisters and make Elise an only child.

Once that was done, I was told that I spent a great deal of time describing the action instead of letting the characters live the action.

My editor gave me a simple rule to follow that redirected my thinking and my writing style: When the heroine walks into the room, have her sit on the silk sofa, cross her long legs, and proudly display her expensive Manolo Blahnik shoes.

In one sentence we know that the heroine is in an expensive house, that she is feminine and proud of it and perhaps a bit sexy, since she crosses her legs, and she has a shoe fetish since she's blown four hundred bucks on a pair of designer shoes. If she lets one shoe fall precariously off the end of her toes, she's really sexy and maybe she's hoping to entice the onlooker.

Change the action a bit.

The heroine throws the library doors back, storms across the wood floor, and plops into a wing chair and looks around the room for an instant. She picks up a ceramic statuette and throws it against the fireplace, where it shatters into a dozen pieces.

This girl is angry, and for anyone to be so angry as to smash objects, the motivator must be something terrible. Perhaps she just discovered her boyfriend is cheating on her. Perhaps she just got fired from her job or her girlfriend betrayed her.

Now let's look at dialogue to tell us about the heroine.

In the first setup, our heroine comes into a beautiful room and sits down. There is no one else in the room. But there will be.

"I thought you'd come."

Our heroine has one line of dialogue that looks simple, but it isn't. Here we learn that she is expecting someone to join her. She has previously set up action to make this meeting occur. Because she has crossed her legs, displaying her very sexy shoes, we expect the person to be a man.

We can discern that the heroine is foxy, smart, manipulative, plotting, possibly desperate, and determined, and she believes that the man entering the room will be attracted to her.

She has said very little and done very little, but already, she has set the scene for something explosive to happen. Our scene could be a passionate love scene. It could be the heroine hoping to make up with her lover who for some reason has been estranged from her. It could even be the heroine simply using her feminine wiles to get a promotion from her boss.

In the second setup, we have a very angry young lady.

Her line would be: "Leave me alone!"

This woman is not only angry; she's hurt and she is afraid to allow someone to get emotionally close. In actuality, she is begging for help. She wants the man coming into the room to comfort her. She wants an explanation for the previous event that will ease her pain. She is feeling about as rotten as a person can. The last thing she wants is to be left alone.

Our heroine is smack-dab in the middle of her epiphany. She is a woman of great emotions; otherwise, she wouldn't be this angry. She cared a great deal about the person or situation that has led her to this anger. Her soul is wounded. She has a problem with trust; thus, her first instinct is to tell the man to go away. Her emotional wounds probably go back to her childhood, and she could be feeling the pain not only of the recent incident but of the past as well.

How uninteresting this scene would be if we used the former line, "I knew you'd come."

She made all this noise to attract a man's attention? What is she, a drama queen? She would need a psychologist, and no hero-worthy character in our book would have anything to do with a woman that messed up. She would reveal herself to be shallow, insincere, a manipulator, and selfish.

If you find yourself struggling to make your dialogue sound realistic, take cues from real people. I know it is impolite, but there are certain circumstances in which eavesdropping is unavoidable. Grocery checkout lines, restaurants, and airports are my favorite. Videos and DVDs are great too, allowing you to watch well-written scenes more than once. When you watch a favorite film, pay very close attention to how the screenwriter uses dialogue. Does it ring true? If so, what about it makes it special to you?

Expanding a bit on what we have just discussed in relation to the heroine, let's look at our hero.

There are a few hard-and-fast rules when it comes to the hero's dialogue.

1. Watch your profanity. Even in erotica, the hero should always be respectful toward the heroine.

2. No verbal abuse. This means that the hero would never be condescending toward the heroine. He would not put her down. He would not call her names. Even in the old "bodice rippers" like Rosemary Rogers made popular in the late 1970s, the hero may rip her clothes off, but he's saying, "My God, I've never seen one like you!"

3. Generally, the hero will not reveal his feelings in dialogue until the end of the story. He can be feeling and thinking all kinds of things, but half the tension of a romance novel is getting the hero to say, "I love you."

There are always exceptions to every rule, but these are the top three when it comes to the hero. The heroine does not share these rules. In fact, she can put the hero down. She can be somewhat abusive to him, but only in the beginning of the story when she doesn't truly know him/understand him. She can call him names, but here, don't be crass or too, too vulgar.

Romantic Dialogue

For a romance author, the idea that language in romances is different than language in mainstream novels can make the skin crawl. We like to think our prose and dialogue is just like that in "real books." The truth is that there really is a difference. The difference is that romances generally are spoken with literally longer phrases.

Flamboyant prose abounds, as do vivid metaphors, but it's in the dialogue where you really see the difference.

"Whatever" has become a single word that describes nothing and yet encompasses everything from frustration to relief.

"I can't take this anymore" is the romantic translation of "whatever."

"I love you." It's said a million times in all fiction and especially romance, but it is stated like the following:

"You mean the world to me. I can't exist without you."

"Once I found you, my life became a symphony."

"Without you there is no reason for me to live."

"When I breathe, I am filled with your essence."

"My heart and your heart. Together we are one and without each other, we cease to exist."

You get the picture. When was the last time someone said any of those things to you? On your wedding night? Ever?

The dialogue of romance is the words a woman wants to hear but seldom does. They are the stuff of dreams. The dialogue needs to be dramatic and romantic, but it is so easy for it to become clunky. The tip here: Just don't overdo it.

If you have the hero saying a long, dramatic line, then keep the heroine's line short and clear.

For a long time, the unspoken romance dialogue rules have been: if you can say it in three sentences rather than two words, go for the long word count.

The thought has always been in romance that the hero and heroine should sound better educated. Your audience is better educated than most readers, so keep that in mind when you are reading.

This is a good time to start expanding your own vocabulary. I used to have to keep a thesaurus by my bedside when I read LaVyrle Spenser's books. Since she retired, I don't have half the fun I used to reading romances. She made me think. And her stories were the best.

In romances, you will need to put into dialogue *what the characters are feeling*. In most novels, the characters don't feel to begin with, so who would care what they are feeling?

Romance characters are all about feelings. The point of their evolution is to get to those feelings and emotions.

The purpose of a good novel is to evoke emotion.

If your romance does not stir emotions, it will never sell. Worse, it won't be remembered.

Those emotions are going to come into play during the dialogue scenes. Whether it is to laugh or cry, the characters must share their sorrows and joys, and they do this by talking to each other.

Vocabulary Specific to Romance

Though I have said this before, the best way to understand romance is to read a lot of them. I've read thousands. Your audience has read tens of thousands. That is not an exaggeration.

The romance novel as we know it today hit its stride in the late 1970s. That is *more than* twenty-five years ago. The average romance reader/addict reads four to five a week. The average romance reader spends upwards of one hundred and twenty dollars a month on her books. Surveys prove that she is not buying all of them at full retail. Some she buys for fifty cents a book at used bookstores. She gets them at the library, she borrows them, and she uses discount cards.

She is reading thirty to sixty books a month. Your reader does not watch television. She reads. She may go to movies with her friends or family, but chances are they have to share the backseat with paperback copies of romance novels she reads at stoplights and on her lunch break at work.

I have met many fans over the years who pride themselves on reading over a thousand books a year. Given that there are over three thousand titles printed in a given year, which are all reviewed by *Romantic Times Magazine*, our favorite reader has a lot of reading yet to do.

Americans have always had a love/hate relationship with sex. At once we are quite puritanical, while our media and advertisements are filled with sex. Look at the hit recording artists and what they wear for their CD dust jackets. Think of Beyoncé or Britney in a turtleneck. It doesn't work. Yet at the same time, stories that Britney had lost her virginity caused shock waves. Our seemingly "open" society is far from it. You must remember this when writing your novel.

Romance novels are very specific when it comes to what is allowed and what is not.

Specifically, you cannot use vulgar descriptions, thoughts, or circumstances in regard to the heroine. She can be feisty and aggressive, even a warrior, but her heart has to be as pure as the driven snow.

The same almost goes for the hero. He can be a rogue in an historical, but steer clear of making him a sexaholic in a contemporary. He can have had lovers, but trust me, he's always been looking for the right woman. He must have all the characteristics that will make *the reader fall in love with him*. He can be graphic when it comes to intimacy, but he cannot be vulgar.

What's the difference?

Vocabulary.

When it comes to romance vocabulary, there are words that have got to be in your manuscript. It doesn't matter how many times your reader has read them; these are the words that help you spin your story.

Besides the obvious word, *love*, the next are: *beautiful, breasts, biceps, engagement* (Joan Rivers coined "bling-bling" for an engagement ring. If writing "chick-lit," I'd use it), *embrace, exotic, erection, fluid, fondle, heart, heat, kiss, passion, pulsating, ripped (as in his muscles), satin, sensual, sensuous, silk, tight, taut, wedding*.

My love scenes are sensual—not graphic, not sexual. I have a trick to my love scenes that I would like to share with you. First, it's not new. I stole the idea from the movie *Tom Jones*. I use food.

There is nothing like a fabulously romantic dinner to set the scene. My old saying is that if love makes the world go around, romance makes it spin. When we think of romance it is simply scene setting. Candlelight dinners, wine, or fabulous icy martinis (oh, Sean Connery, where are you tonight?) arranged on snowy linens on a balcony terrace high above the lights of Manhattan and a single red rose resting on our heroine's gold-rimmed bone china plate will get your reader's heart pumping.

The next thing she wants to know is, "How far is the bedroom?"

Once in the bedroom, I have another trick to my love scenes, and most of the trick is in the vocabulary. I use little action of what is going on, other than what you want to use to create passion. The kiss is more important than the foreplay and the foreplay is more important than the sex, but the climax is ultra-important in my books.

I write a great deal, sometimes ten pages of what is going on in the protagonists' heads.

That vocabulary is quite spiritual, and this is what makes my characters memorable.

Adore, angel, cherish, destiny, diaphanous, divine, earth, fate, flower, heaven, magic, magical, miracle, mist, mystical, moon, paradise, planet, protector, safe harbor, stars, sailing (as in *sailing through the stars), spirit, soul, soul mate, treasure, twin flame, wings, worship.*

This is only a smattering, but you get the idea. Even if our couple breaks up later and gets back together, these are the pure thoughts in their heads. You have not only hooked the reader into the most intimate thoughts in the hero's mind and the heroine's head, but you have clearly shown that these two people will end up together at the end. It's the "how" of getting them there that makes your novel so interesting.

Always remember that a romance novel is about the courtship of the protagonists. They may go through hell (hopefully) to get together, but the end result must be the engagement and/or the marriage.

In our social culture and these historic times in which we are living, marriage, commitment, and family are highlighted in life like never before. Even a hundred years ago our agrarian forefathers struggled every day to put food on the table. Life was survival and there probably wasn't much time for love or relationships. If you ask our grandparents, most of them say, "We were just trying to survive." They didn't think much about the psychology of their relationships. A woman married a man to have a roof over her head and food on the table. If he became a father to the children she wanted to have, so much the better.

At the core of every romance novel is the belief by the author, the publisher, and the reader that a loving relationship is at the core of every human family.

Remembering all these factors will help you choose your romance vocabulary.

Thus, the "hot" words for contemporary romance are the ones we have been using for decades: *engagement, ring, wedding, marriage, commitment, pledge, vows,* and *home.* The romance is about the courtship. The "happy ending" is about the wedding itself or the happy marriage at the conclusion.

Your reader did not buy your novel to be disappointed. She bought it to be uplifted at the end, and to her, that means the boy and girl get together in the end with some form of commitment. As long as that engagement is implied or the marriage is implied, to the reader, it is still a happy ending.

Use your genius to take these words and use them in your prose:

Hero: "I found my home in you."

Heroine: "Our hearts have long been wed."

These lines are both historically applicable and contemporary. Using vocabulary specific to romance is an obvious must, but for fun, here is a contemporary list of words with its historical equivalent.

Historical

- ✤ Love
- ✤ Rapture
- ✤ Beautiful
- ✤ Fevered
- ✤ Passionate
- ✤ Voluptuous
- ✤ Masterful
- ✤ Unmarried
- ✤ Bachelor
- ✤ Rogue
- ✤ Connected (socially)
- ✤ Proposal
- ✤ Debutante
- ✤ Steamy
- ✤ Debonair
- ✤ Charming
- ✤ Attractive
- ✤ Sexy
- ✤ Sex
- ✤ Married

Contemporary

✤ Love

✤ Zoned

✤ Awesome

✤ Hot

✤ Fired up

✤ Sexy/profiles

✤ Practiced

✤ Singleton

✤ Commitment phobic

✤ One-nighter/networked/online

✤ Hooked in

✤ Pop the question/propose

✤ Virgin (back in fashion)

✤ Steamy

✤ Smooth

✤ Con artist

✤ Magnetic

✤ Pervy

✤ Shag

✤ Married

Many of our current "in vogue" dialogue is being borrowed from England. You will start seeing more and more British slang used in books and films. You'll hear it in restaurants from very young girls and young women. Check out the popular talk shows, and you'll hear this jargon from young actresses. It is certainly in the Working Title productions such as *Bridget Jones's Diary* and *Love, Actually.* In the years to come, we will be seeing more British vocabulary moving into our culture, and it's here to stay.

Twenty years ago, French phrases were all the fashion. Now they are outré. So are Italian phrases, and to me, nothing is more endearing than "cara mia." Can't you just picture the tall, dark hero calling?

Spanish vocabulary is moving in with a vengeance, as is the Hispanic audience. You would be wise to watch this market. There are over eleven million Hispanic women in the United States buying romance novels. They love them.

I have been using Hispanic dishes and recipes for years, along with my favorite phrases. I lived in Ecuador for three years, so my base of research for this is strong. You don't have to move to a foreign country to expand your vocabulary, but don't be afraid to use the remote control on your television and watch Univision or Telemundo programming sometimes. Try to write an Hispanic heroine for fun. Think of Salma Hayek as your Spanish heroine. She's a fine actress. Antonio Banderas isn't bad either for the hero.

One caution when you are gleaning the latest hip-hop records and watching movies for inspiration. What works in those industries does not work in romance writing. Not long ago I was handed a manuscript by a middle-aged writer who thought that her romance was just what the public wanted. It was filled with so much garbage vocabulary; I had a very difficult time digging down to the story. No surprise, there wasn't one—at least not one that readers of romance novels wanted.

We will get into sub-genres of romance, including erotica, but even in erotica, there is no room for garbage.

Creating Believable Subplots

Even in category romance, you will have a small subplot, usually only enough either to bring the couple together or to be used as a device to break them up. There should not be much time spent on a category subplot. The action and the story line should revolve as much as possible around the couple.

Because there are so many sub-genres in romance today, the use of the subplot is almost assured.

The trick to making subplots believable is to use real-life situations as your story line. Twenty years ago, editors admonished us not to use clichés. Today, the word bandied about is "predictable." The problem is that the clichés are the things that are so real-life. You can use them, but use them cautiously. If your subplot is too outrageous or just doesn't make sense, it will clang against the main story line and the result will not be the symphony you seek.

Romances are rife with misunderstandings, gossip, lies, treachery, and miscommunication. Frankly, they are the basis of all good soap operas. And soap operas sell.

Therefore, to make even the clichés work, remember to keep your story line as natural as possible. Don't have characters and plot twists coming in out of left field. Start out with an idea, lay clues to what will happen in the future, and then slowly reveal the truth in the ending chapters.

Foreshadowing is very important in all the mystery, thriller, suspense, paranormal, and even fantasy romances. Simply use a light hand when you reveal plots.

In my book *Wings of Destiny*, my main plot was the love affair between Jefferson Duke and Caroline Mansfield. Jefferson, a blonde-haired, green-eyed mulatto slave who has escaped from a plantation in Carolina, passes himself off as white once he comes to San Francisco in 1832. He begins his life there as a trapper and hunter. During those early years the land is owned by the Spanish Dons.

Dolores Sanchez falls in love with Jefferson, but he never returns her love. She is incredibly beautiful and very headstrong. Her father actually locks her in her room so that she will not pursue Jefferson. Over the years, Dolores becomes an alcoholic.

Jefferson falls in love with Caroline, who is already married, and she refuses to get a divorce.

Dolores discovers Jefferson's affair with Caroline, and in a drunken rage, she goes to Caroline's weak-willed husband, William, hoping to break Jefferson and Caroline apart. But the plan backfires, because William knows all about his wife's affair. He knows that she considers her deathbed promise to her father that she marry William to be sacred. William, a bitter, spiteful, hate-filled man, would rather spend his life keeping Caroline from happiness and living a lie than allow her to be free.

Stunned, Dolores rushes out into the rainy night. A bolt of lightning frightens her horse and Dolores is killed that night.

This is a strong subplot.

Dolores's obsession with Jefferson takes up a good deal of the book, and until the night she dies, she creates havoc for our hero and heroine. Until the night of the storm when Dolores dies, the reader believes that William knows nothing of Caroline's love for Jefferson. The reader actually feels a bit sorry for William until his true identity is revealed.

This revelation is accomplished in the subplot story line about Dolores. There is no confrontation between Caroline and William, or between Jefferson and William.

Until this point, William portrays himself as a vapid, uninteresting storekeeper who is half the businessperson that his wife is. He has no courage, no pride, and stays to himself most of the story.

However, there are tiny foreshadowings that point to the anger that he harbors. These are revealed in offhanded comments in his dialogue. Always use subtlety when writing this kind of reveal, but in a romance especially, these lines of dialogue can be wondrously effective.

Building in Backstory

All stories have some backstory. There are no rules about how much is enough. You need what you need to tell your story intelligently. You should have enough information to round out the heroine's personality. If her family is dead and she has no one, then at least give some family history. If you keep the family as part of the story, little anecdotes about Sally's childhood can come out in dialogue.

When you tell these stories, make certain that the childhood experience she had when she fell off the horse is pertinent later in the story or is essential to her character development.

Do not give background details for either the hero or heroine that don't go anywhere. There should be a reason for everything you write.

Sub-genres will require significantly more backstory because we need to know why the heroine is being stalked and who would want to do this to her; why she is living on this alien planet; or why there is an element of mystery, suspense around her.

Most backstory will come into play in Act I, but not all of it. You will need some of the story in the first chapter about the hero or the heroine and then you can dribble a bit more out in the following couple of chapters. Then stop there.

The rest of the backstory should be saved until the final unveiling of the evil plot against the heroine in the last chapter or second to last chapter.

Backstory answers the question *why*. You will need to give enough information to answer some of that question in the beginning, but leave the kicker until the end.

Your plot will determine whose backstory, the hero's or the heroine's, that will be more important. If the hero is the one who must come around to opening his heart, then you might want to save the cause of his lack of trust until the end reveal, when you tell his childhood story of being abandoned by his mother in a foreign country and making his way to the American embassy in Prague at the age of ten by himself.

Or . . . you may want to reveal this in the first Act so that you create empathy for the hero right off the bat.

Use your plotline to help guide you when it comes to whose backstory deserves more pages and attention.

Creating a Strong Supporting Cast

The minimal supporting cast is found in a "category romance." Here you will need a girlfriend/mother/aunt/sister/father/cousin/brother/male buddy to be her "mirror." It is to this person that she confides her love for the hero and her misgivings. This "mirror" will then give guidance and wisdom.

The hero should have a "mirror," as well, but it is not as important as the heroine's "mirror."

Once you move into sub-genres, especially mystery, suspense, and thrillers, the list can be as long as you need it to be to create the kind of story you want.

The average reader can easily keep track of half a dozen major characters. If you start moving beyond that, it can be confusing to them. If you want and need this much supporting cast, then give those characters clearly defined characteristics. Make their dialogue so unique, the reader can always tell who is talking.

The hero and heroine should dominate the story, but that doesn't mean they never interact with anyone else. Half to two thirds of the page count should be that of the heroine and hero, if not even more in a sub-genre or mainstream book.

If your intrigue is really involved, you may have everyone from detectives to heads of state getting page time in your book. Except when you are showing the evil villain in his lair with his cohorts, the hero or the heroine must be center stage, interacting with the supporting cast or with each other.

Editing and Revising Your Work

The editing and revision of your work is a personal choice. Some authors want to wait until the entire manuscript is finished before they revise. For others, editing happens after every sentence.

As a beginner, you should at least edit at the end of every chapter. If you have started to wander off-story, you will catch your problems before they escalate.

It is a good habit to try to edit after each paragraph, but for too many writers, this would slow them down.

When you first begin editing yourself, look for the obvious:

❧ Check your dialogue. Does it sound clunky?

❧ Check your facts. Editors hate unfounded comments.

❧ Do your paragraphs flow from one to the other?

❧ Are you TELLING the story and not showing it?

❧ Are the pages all narrative? If so, alter them into scenes of dialogue and action. Never tell the story when you can show it.

Mistakes the Romance Editor Hates

Romance editors can spot a new writer in two pages. The reason is because new authors write in narrative. This is the single greatest kiss of death. This is what we mean by telling the story and not showing it.

If you can, start your story with an action scene. One sentence to describe the physical area and then go right into a line of dialogue from the hero or the heroine's mouth.

Check your spelling. Typos. Grammar. Paginate.

Put your manuscript on clean paper, double spaced, one sided, and don't bind it. You can't imagine how many times new authors are told this and they never do it! No wonder editors get frustrated. Read the directions! Clean paper, double spaced, one sided, unbound manuscript.

Hiring a Freelance Editor to Review Your Work Prior to Submission

There are former publishing house editors who now will read for a fee and give a small critique. You can hire a "full edit," which costs a substantial amount of money if done by a career professional. If you truly believe you have a book that is superior and you are passionate about getting published, this may be the way to go for you.

This work, however, is likely to cost hundreds of dollars. For your money, you should ask for a full-line edit, help, assistance on a query letter and submission package, and even career advice from this professional.

If your book is good enough, this professional author, former editor, working editor, or former agent may offer to "place" you within their agency or connect you to their connections in publishing. You cannot put a dollar amount on this kind of aid and advice. Inside the head of that former editor is so much knowledge, experience, and hard-knock "inside the industry" information that you would never acquire if you had not hired this person to work with you.

You can find such editors' advertisements listed in writing magazines and digests. If you go to a writer's conference, usually affiliated with local universities, you may find published authors and professional editors who will read "on the side."

One note of caution: Unfortunately, scams and cons exist in every business, and they do exist in romance publishing. To avoid this, if you find an editorial person with whom you wish to work, ask them for references.

In the reputable writer's magazines, most people who advertise to edit are legitimate. If you pick up the local paper and see this kind of ad, it's probably bogus.

When you do find an editor, ask if they have references. They should have a list of former clients or letters of recommendation.

In times past, you could spot the cons a mile away because they always charged a great deal of money to read your book. These days, that's not so true. The prices have gone up considerably, but you get what you pay for.

For a simple edit, grammar, and no story consultation, the price should be under a hundred dollars.

If you are getting story consultation and if your manuscript is really a mess, the price could be up to a thousand dollars. When the price gets this high, essentially, you are hiring someone to write your book for you. Thought of in those terms, it's a bargain.

If you think the price is too much, ask them to outline on paper what it is that they are providing for their services. If they have a contract to sign, so much the better. In that contract should be a clear explanation of the services.

If you want more than they provide—perhaps more aid with the storytelling rather than just the grammar and awkward sentences—then ask them how much extra that should cost.

The good editors are the ones who have worked in publishing as editors, agents, or writers. To hire a college graduate is not to get that wealth of knowledge that comes from working with someone who knows what is selling.

A former editor or another author will supply you with new plots that work better and can help you truly create characters that jump off the page.

Some editors will offer you a sample chapter of their work. This is not common, but it is done.

If you have the chance to go to Romance Writers of America's convention every year, there are dozens of agents and editors who attend these conferences. Go to their workshops. Listen to the authors who speak on writing. After you take notes, go up afterward and ask if they hire out to edit. You just may be surprised at the answer.

SEVEN

Plotting the Memorable Meet

$\mathcal{H}$ow the hero and the heroine get together is termed "the meet" in romantic fiction. It is the single most important plotting device to the genre, and it is a measure of the author's creativity by the editor as to whether she or he is going to buy your book.

Now that you have spent hours, days, and months devising this "super" man and this adorable, vivacious heroine so that to you, they are living, breathing people, you must make certain they meet in a way that no human has ever thought about meeting before. At least, this is what agents and editors tell us at workshops, seminars, and national conventions.

Sound impossible? Don't worry. It isn't. Actually, your hero will meet the woman of his dreams in much the same way that men have always met women, but in a romance, their meeting must be "set up" and given a twist or something very spicy.

The Twist Meet

In this process of setting up the characters, the author must use the hero's attitudes either "for" or "against" the heroine.

Let's say you are writing an historical novel. You want the hero to be a rogue, a dyed-in-the-wool freedom lover. Our hero, Pierre, swears he is never going to fall in love, much less get married. His male friends, pirate buddies or even cellmates, admire him because he appears bigger than life to them. He is not vulnerable, committed, or tied down, as his friends appear to be, to a wife or children. He appears on the surface to have it all. The hero can even be a bit of a braggart, though don't get too heavy on this, or you will never conjure any sympathy for him later.

What we have done here is set up our hero for "the fall." He is cocksure that he will never succumb to a woman's tricks; that he will never be made a fool by love; and that, most importantly, *he* is in control of his life. Perhaps he is proud of this fact. Perhaps he lords his ability to control the fates over his compatriots.

Enter our heroine, Angela. She is beautiful, of course, especially in historical romances; beauty is a requisite attribute for our girl. She is also nobody's fool and she speaks her mind, since little of that was done hundreds of years ago. Women were seen but not heard. The women who were heard made history.

When the hero meets the heroine, don't have her riding on a runaway horse, carriage, or buckboard. Those chase scenes are overdone. If you must use a chase scene, save it for later in the book when it would be fun to have her save him from falling over the cliff or losing control of the reins. It is best to treat these twists with humor in order to keep the hero up on that pedestal.

Spicy Meets

Equally familiar is the scene where the hero spies on the heroine bathing. Whether she is nude in a lagoon, in a tub in a log cabin on the prairie, in a waterfall, or under an outdoor shower under a rain barrel, this scene is as old as time and it will never be overdone.

Naked works.

However, we want a twist to our spicy meet to make it even more fun and saleable. One of my favorite "meets" is the hero coming to the contemporary heroine's front door as a Western Union messenger, singing happy birthday to her in his birthday suit. Think how cute that would be if he did that in the Old West or at her cabin door aboard a ship. Perhaps the entire pirate crew sees him singing naked in the corridor and then they joke with him for days about it. The hero believes he is losing his authority over his men and blames our heroine.

Where is our hero's pride now? Precisely. Now we've set up a plot in which the hero has to prove himself over and over again, not just to the heroine, but also to the crew or his friends.

In a romance, it's all right to poke fun at our characters once, maybe twice, but that is all. Now that we have our fabulous, handsome, rugged man being laughed at by his subordinates, the plot takes on a new dimension. Let's say the first mate on the ship has been jealous of our hero for years. This is the first crack he's seen in our hero's armor, and he's going for it.

Our villain sets up all kinds of pitfalls for the hero, including trying to break up the lovebirds. If he can use Angela to cause our hero to give up the seas, or better, die, then the first mate can take over the ship, confiscate all our hero's treasures and if he's really lucky, bamboozle the girl into falling for him. Make the villain really handsome and a great actor, and you have a multitude of conflicts and triangles.

All that, and all we did was to take the guy's clothes off!

Conflict as a Background

Truly great meets are set against incredible strife. War is great for this. To best illustrate my points, I will use both film and novel titles and themes because the classic films are so universally recognized. *Casablanca, Pearl Harbor, A Farewell to Arms,* and *Gone with the Wind* were all set against the background of war. War heightens the tension, creates extraordinary circumstances the characters must overcome and in a historical setting, creates an intrinsic timeline that aids in pace and suspense. These aforementioned films are some of the most memorable love stories of all time, but look at how our heroes and heroines met.

In *Casablanca*, Rick and Ilsa had met in Paris, yes. But it was when she walked through the door in his bar in Morocco. His heart had been bleeding for her for years and had nearly healed over. Then, all she had to do was show up again and we have combustion.

The Reunion Meet

One of the most memorable introductions of characters is the "reunion meet." This theme is the one that requires considerable backstory. The idea is that our couple should have worked things out a long time ago and didn't. Something happened that kept them apart and they never dealt with it, usually because they were too afraid. When they do see each other again, that past, both the sweet and sour, is right up there in their faces and ours. The author has set up conflict and tension just by having this couple meet again.

Think of other ways to do the above. The high school reunion is being done a lot lately, but there are other, ramped-up reunions. What about a hero and heroine who had known each other as children and don't even remember each other? Then they are brought together at a family reunion and they are instantly attracted to each other. Perhaps their parents are dead, but Uncle Andy and Auntie Rita tell them they are cousins. For weeks they "fight" this growing friendship and passion, date others, and everything falls apart. Finally, in the end, they find out they aren't related at all. The author could take a very humorous run with this, setting all kinds of hilarious sequences together. Or the author could go the tragic romance path and create a real tearjerker.

Though the story was set against the backdrop of the Civil War, Scarlett met Rhett at a neighbor's barbeque. That's the bottom line, but it was the way he looked at her that annoyed her first, and then challenged her, and that look has caused generations to read this book and see the movie repeatedly. The author, Margaret Mitchell, made us ride a very long roller coaster before Scarlett woke up and realized she really did love Rhett, but by then it was too late. Or was it?

Love at First Sight Meet

This "love at first sight" theme is part and parcel of the memorable meet plotting.

Some of my favorite meets I've gleaned from real life. I have a married couple that I've known for nearly a decade. The story of how they met is classic boy sees girl and is "hooked." Roger was out sailing in the Gulf of Mexico south of Galveston one Sunday afternoon, and as the sun was setting and the boats were sailing back to their respective docks, Roger saw a very large boat coming alongside the boat he was on. Pulling the topsail down was a blonde young woman wearing a bright lime green bikini. He was stunned watching her, thinking how beautiful she was. As if reading his thoughts, Anne stopped working and looked over to the sailboat, and saw Roger, and across that vast distance, their eyes met. She smiled and waved to him as her boat moved ahead of his. Roger would have paddled their boat to the dock in order not to miss Anne. He turned to his friend and said, "See that girl? I'm going to marry that girl."

Of course, everyone on board laughed at him. Roger's boat got to the dock well after Anne's boat was tied up and she'd left. He asked all over the dock about this girl, but she was "a friend of a friend." Two weeks later, Roger walked into a restaurant in Houston and saw what he thought was the same girl. He dashed up to her and asked if she had been sailing two weeks prior and was wearing a green bikini. Anne smiled and assured him she was that girl.

They made arrangements to have dinner the next night, and from that moment, they were inseparable. Today they have been married over twenty-five years.

"Love at first sight" meets happen in real life all the time. Placing them against wartime or natural disasters broadens the canvas for the writer.

Going back to our wartime backdrop, in the movie *Pearl Harbor*, both our heroes meet the woman of their dreams basically with their pants down. The heroine is the induction nurse administering injections, thus the dropping trou scene, and the twist in this meet is that the woman has the power over our hero as to whether he will pass his eye exam and be allowed to fulfill his dream of becoming a pilot. The writer's wisdom of turning the tables of control to the woman's favor not only "archs" the heroine, but dramatizes the hero's vulnerability and makes the audience sympathetic to both characters, thus drawing the audience deeply into the story.

The Cute Meet

"Cute meets" by definition are almost always used in the contemporary vein, but there are plenty for the historical writer as well. Even in real life, people "bump" into each other, and from the first moment of contact, something goes "zing."

A woman wanders into a chat room online and so does a man. They exchange e-mails and the next thing you know, *You've Got Mail* is born. During the Christmas holiday season, a man reaches for a black glove at Bloomingdale's to buy for his girlfriend at precisely the same moment a young woman grabs the same glove. Their meeting is prophetic, though not for several years. This is the premise of the movie *Serendipity*. When you think of it, all they did to meet was "bump" into each other. Whether you believe they were brought together by chance or fate is the exploration of the author.

One of the best "cute meets" in moviedom is *Sleepless in Seattle*, in which a woman hears a man's voice on the radio and falls in love with his grieving soul and his caring and concerned eight-year-old son.

Everyday or Work-Related Meets

"Everyday meets" are seemingly ordinary, plausible everyday circumstances in which two people come together. In one of the romance novels I have loved, the author had the hero delivering a bed to the heroine. My heroine in *Tender Malice* tried to sell the hero her new computer program. He wasn't buying . . . for awhile, anyway. Heroes have met their leading ladies everywhere from the jungles of Colombia, as in *Romancing the Stone*, to the asphalt jungles of Manhattan board rooms as in Judith Krantz's *Scruples*.

Taking the ordinary meeting and creating that haunting moment that stays in the reader's mind for weeks, and hopefully forever, is where the magic of your talent is revealed.

Going back to our hero who delivered the bed to the heroine, let's analyze several plot twists that will make the story more intriguing than just the feelings inside the heroine's heart and go beyond the sexy thoughts in the hero's head. (I am not using the plot of the original author's story here.)

Let's say that our girl—Tuesday, we will call her—has a very small apartment in Brooklyn, where it can be pretty dangerous in areas. She is a butcher, so she's feisty in spirit and athletic in body. She was brought up with eight sisters and they lived on top of each other all her life. This is her first taste of real freedom. Her own apartment, her own room. Thus this magnificent king-sized, ironwork bed frame, mattress, and springs represent power, control, and success to her. It's a magical bed.

She bought the bed at Bloomingdale's. Our hero is working as a deliveryman but he's really just breaking into acting. He pulls up into the alley outside her three-story walk-up apartment, and gets a call on his cell that he just landed a huge Broadway lead. It's the moment of his life. He's not thinking about this bed he is delivering.

You get the picture. He does everything wrong. The bed won't fit up the stairway. He has to get it up to the third floor using pulleys. Maybe the rope breaks. He drops the bed. It is destroyed and our hero will do anything to get to the meeting with his agent.

Tuesday is arguing with him. She is furious. They argue, with him threatening to walk off the job to get to his meeting. Finally, she makes him tell her what is going on and after he explains, she agrees to drive him to his meeting if he will come back and deliver the bed properly. Once we see them actually communicating, we realize that somehow they will work this thing out. Plus we have set up the sexual tension around the bed and its "initiation." We can't wait to get them into the bed.

Conflict Meets

Perhaps the "cute meet" isn't your style. You want to write a more serious story with a broad canvas, but not necessarily war. These stories tend to be contemporary and use backdrops of women working for the CIA, large and powerful corporations, or socially conscious international organizations in which the heroine is fighting for the rights of the underprivileged.

These "conflict meets" between the hero and heroine are most intriguing when the hero is against the heroine's cause, country, or company, and she must fight all obstacles, including his dark and closed heart. This is the kind of heroine that must make a case for herself, and in the process, she wins the hero to her side. Courtroom romances like those of author, Laura Van Wormer best exemplify this kind of "internal" and "external" war going on. The courtroom is a great place for two characters to meet. They can be the jurors and thrown into a trial that involves isolation and noninvolvement in the rest of their ordinary lives. You could twist things all over the place and have the heroine be the judge and the hero is the accused.

Here is a tool I've devised to help me out when I'm trying to come up with stories, and though it started just for fun, it's rather handy. Once you have decided that you want to write a courtroom romance or a hospital romance, for instance, on small pieces of paper place the names of the expected figureheads on each piece. For the courtroom we would have the judge, the bailiff, the prosecuting attorney, the defending attorney, the accused, the witnesses, the jurors, and maybe a cop or two and some expert witnesses. By assigning male roles to some of the figureheads, you can begin to play with this process. In traditionally male roles, use females. In some of the male roles—don't stretch too much here—romantic audiences like their men to be masculine; reverse the genders and have a man be the expert witness as the psychotherapist, perhaps.

In a hospital romance I am writing titled *Beauty's Beast*, I have the heroine as the plastic surgeon who puts the hero's face back together. She creates a face that she falls in love with. The hero, Jack, has no memory of the shooting or any of his past leading up to the shooting, but he does know in his soul he would never try to kill himself, as the police claim.

A word here about device of amnesia. Every time I think the amnesia theme has been overworked, some brilliant author comes along and proves me wrong. Loss of memory through brain tumors, accidents, disease, etc., is here to stay. Frankly, I believe it's part science and part fiction. The human brain is the last frontier. We know so little about it and in that fact, we are all fascinated with what our human capabilities truly are and are not.

In *Beauty's Beast*, the twist is that the reason Jack can't remember why on earth he would want to kill himself is because he *did not* try to commit suicide. The attempted murder was planned by his unfaithful wife and her lover, Jack's business partner, in order to inherit his businesses. Jack foiled their plans by living through the gunshot. Our heroine, Sally, not only rebuilds Jack's face, but she falls in love with her "beast" and together, they bring the would-be murderers to justice. Thus, in this story line, the "meet" is critical to the entire plot.

In contemporary novels the "meets" have a wide canvas of possibilities. Do not overlook dating services, meeting at the green room on *The Tonight Show with Jay Leno*, or even in the audience of a game show; online chat rooms, in a church group or bereavement group; in physical therapy as well as a rehab center; at the lottery winner's office, and on and on. Between the newspaper, entertainment magazines, and her own personal habits, the talented author can take even a meeting at a street crossing light and make sparks fly.

Historical Meets

Historical meetings must, at all costs, take into account the society and the customs of the age. If your heroine were in Spain in the 1800s she would have a duenna. If she were in France in the 1700s she would have a chaperone unless she is a woman of the streets, which sets up an entirely different kind of meet. Always research your characters' geographic local, religious, and cultural mores. You can still have fun and create scintillating meetings by bending mores a bit. In my book, *Seduced*, the very proper heroine meets the man of her dreams in the streets of Venice during Mardi Gras. He is wearing a mask and so is she. She manipulates society's rule that a lady should be escorted to the max, and defiantly she slips away from a very proper ball, alone, in order to sow a few wild oats the night before her betrothal to a man she has never met. She thinks.

Historical romance meets include the following: the arranged betrothal (not engagement) or marriage; "proper" introductions through family or well-meaning friends; deathbed promises by a dying male parent to a hand-picked or favorite relative, guardian, lord, or suitor to marry his daughter, and thus, in return, the new fiancé will inherit all our heroine's property.

The plot device in historicals in which the heroine inherits a large house and is forced to live in that house and thus she meets the hero upon her move, is called the gothic romance.

This type of meet involving inherited property is an old device, and though I used it over fifteen years ago in *All or Nothing*, unless you blend other genres like the supernatural or science fiction with romance, editors tend to turn a deaf ear to such meets and plots today.

If the heroine of the historical romance is not wealthy, the author has access to more meets. The poor heroine is not bound by any rules. She can be a spy for the Confederate Army, a dancehall girl, a nurse, a slave, a teacher, a gunslinger, a businesswoman, a pirate, and an explorer of new territory.

Though we may not have the hero bump into our heroine as we do in contemporary romances, these meets are a bit more strategized from the outset and take a great deal more plotting prior to the meet.

In an historical setting, use history to dictate your characters' meeting. Remember the great ones? Anthony and Cleopatra? He came to conquer her nation. Or Napoleon and Josephine? She was his favorite at court. I wrote an historical set against World War I in which my hero, Christopher Mann, spied on Elise Kendall sitting on a porch in a white linen dress. At first glance it appears that our hero is simply admiring a pretty woman. Actually, he was sent by a subversive group to marry her and take her to Europe as a front for espionage purposes. His participation was part of the force behind the "Black Hand" terrorist group that murdered Archduke Francis Ferdinand, the "shot that was heard around the world."

Using a famous historical character to introduce the two main characters is such great fun for the author. In *Wings of Destiny*, I used President Theodore Roosevelt as hero Michael Trent's employer to introduce the heroine, Barbara, to Michael. Being able to put words into a president's mouth is truly an adrenaline rush for the author. Do not be afraid to play with history a little, but make certain your audience will always know when you are turning fact into fiction. The actual instances of historic battles, political situations, natural disasters, and the like must be thoroughly documented. Your editor will ask you for backup and you must be ready to provide it.

Even though you have used kings and potentates to introduce the hero and heroine, it is essential in most historical romances that the hero be bigger than life. If you choose to use a factual historical person such as a prince or pirate, make certain that the hero has a personality that is more interesting, daring, and endearing than the historical persons in the plot. The hero doesn't need to be wealthy, per se; remember that in that time frame that was important to his attractiveness as a hero because men were measured by their ability to provide well for a wife and their—hopefully—many children.

As a general rule, historical romances work best when the heroine must lean on the man to save her either physically from harm's way or from an intrigue being built around the two of them by either his or her enemies within the court, society, or feuding tribes/clansmen. I have a couple of favorite authors who have written interesting romances in which the heroine was the pirate, the gunslinger, the Old West bounty hunter, the Old West marshall, and even a Civil War blockade runner. To date I haven't seen a male hero and female heroine meet in an historical on the actual battlefield fighting hand-to-hand combat, but wouldn't that be intriguing?

Once the characters have met, the conflict between the two main characters comes when they realize their lives or their closed hearts, neurosis, or life challenges just don't mesh. Thus when they meet during the haunting interlude scene you, the author, have created, something inside the hero and heroine tells one or both of them to resist this love they feel. It takes a lot of courage to love, which is the reason it is the greatest challenge for a human, and it takes even more strength, openness, and generosity to give one's heart to another. Despite the fact that our hero has met his lady love, the reader knows that boy must lose girl, then either he or the heroine must get his or her act together and/or save a good part of the known world before they can truly be together again in bliss and harmony.

EIGHT

Writing the Love Scene

*I*n a romance novel, the love scenes are one of the most critical pieces of writing you will do. Be assured that your audience not only wants these scenes in the book, but they are paying very good money to the authors who deliver them well.

Love Scenes and "Head Action"

The action, dialogue, and pacing in the love scenes are unbelievably important.

Again, you will need to refer back to or keep in mind the sub-genre you are writing.

If this is a spiritual- or religious-based story, your love scene is not going to be graphic in detail. Your dialogue is not going to hint at anything racy or spicy. You will want to keep the Victoria's Secret underwear in the drawer, but that does not mean that your characters would be prudes, either. There is nothing more beautiful than the human body.

No matter what the genre of romance you have chosen, your hero and heroine should always have respect for each other in bed. Their dialogue will be loving at all times.

They can have fun and kid around, but loving respect is what makes a hero and a heroine.

Even in the raciest love scenes you can write, the best part of the scene is what is going on in the heads of the protagonists.

It is best to break the love scene down into four parts.

First is the kiss.

Second in the love scene is the proposition of sex.

Third is the sexual act.

Fourth is the action after the lovemaking.

The kiss is the most romantic part of the romance. The action, dialogue, and backstory all lead up to when the hero will kiss the heroine. The next block of action leads up to when the hero will kiss the heroine again. If you've ever read a Judith McNaught romance, you know what a great kiss should be like. Judith writes fabulous kissing scenes.

In hers and any good kissing scene there is a lot that the characters think about and react to as they kiss each other.

The kiss is considered by many to be more intimate than the sexual act. The kiss is sharing, caring, and it is sweet. Your choice of how you want to execute the first kiss between your protagonists will depend on their character. Should it be quick and impulsive? Anticipated? Filled with love? Filled with regret? Blatantly humorous? The options for the kiss are endless.

The kiss is an end in itself. It does not have to lead to anything more than what it is. The decision for the action of the characters to go beyond the kiss will be determined by the characters themselves and what the kiss means to them and its placement in their lives.

If you ever saw *Last Tango in Paris*, the movie set the cinema world on its ear because two strangers in Paris have sex in the first scene. They don't even know each other's names, but they have sex. The rest of the movie then reveals who these people are.

Half the romance movies ever made and most westerns don't have a kiss until the last scene, when the cowboy gets the girl and rides off into the sunset with her.

The placement of the kiss then depends on the characters and their development.

The second part of action in the love scene is the proposition of sex. This can be implied and it does not have to have culmination to be effective. In the movie *French Kiss*, the Meg Ryan character is forced to sleep in the same hotel room as Kevin Kline. For a brief moment we believe there might be a proposition of sex between them because the setting itself (the hotel room on the French Riviera) sets us up to believe Kevin will propose to have sex with Meg. Instead, Kevin leans over the bed, takes a bed pillow, and then lies down on the couch on the other side of the room.

In your novel, you could write a romantic comedy by using the proposition of sex being ever present, but the main characters can never find a place or time to be intimate. The quest could be hilarious and frustrating, and yet it would finally have to end with the third part of the love scene structure, the sexual act.

During the sexual act itself is when you must use more than the details of lovemaking to make your story interesting. This is when you can reveal a great deal about who your characters really are.

The heroine might be a virgin. If this is her first time to make love, is she married? Single? Is she in love or just experimenting? Is this a magical experience? Or does she wish she were shopping instead?

As a general rule, for most of the love making scene you will want to stay in the heroine's head. It is her reaction to him that we are most interested in. It is through her heart and her eyes that the reader is experiencing the story.

You will need to have some of the head action be in the hero's head, but it should be kept to no more than a third.

I remember writing a love scene in which I literally split the head thoughts fifty-fifty between the hero and the heroine. My editor quickly let me know that that was not the way to do it.

There are times when you might want to have all the head action in the hero's head to garner empathy for him or to reveal elements of his character that he has kept hidden from the heroine. This is a good place to do it.

The *dialogue* in the love scene can be funny, moving, loving, tender, and even hot. Never make the mistake that this is the place for profanity. It will get edited out.

I have always used the rule that if I even use profanity, it should come out of the mouths of the villains.

Most of the dialogue in love scenes is saved for the *aftermath*. At this point you can have your hero, if he's a commitment-phobe like Billy Crystal in *When Harry Met Sally*, jump out of bed and race home.

Or, it is a good time for the hero to reveal his deep devotion out loud to the heroine.

There are no hard-and-fast rules about this. I've heard advice that the hero should never reveal his love until the very last scenes so that the heroine is kept guessing.

I have also read some great romances in which the hero tells the heroine that he loves her in the very first pages and it takes the entire book for the two to get together and finally have a life together. Frankly, this last one sounds like real life, doesn't it?

The structure of the love scene is laid in stone.

The placement of the love scene probably depends on the sub-genre you are writing.

The execution of the love scene is what defines the tone of your work and may be the yardstick by which your readers measure you.

The love scene is the internal combustion of the romance. Your reader picked a romance because she expects there to be a romance. If he/she wanted a straight mystery, that's what they would buy. The love scene is the most difficult scene to write as you move from your first novel to the tenth. Keeping your dialogue fresh and the action exciting is challenging, because lovemaking has specific elements and there are no surprises for the reader.

Your choice of vocabulary, the scene setup, the physical surroundings, and then the characters' emotional reactions after the sex act are what make your work unique and memorable.

For example:

George closed the door with his foot, balancing a tray holding two glasses of champagne. "I brought you something," he whispered to sleeping Janet.

Opening her eyes, she pushed down the cream-colored satin sheet enough to lift her hand. She took the crystal flute, smiled wickedly, and then pushed the sheet past her naked breasts, down to her abdomen. Slowly, she poured the champagne between her breasts. "Wanna toast?"

This is a cute setup. The dialogue is tight and minimal, but the action is playful and spicy without being glaringly erotic.

These two characters are familiar with each other and there is no tension. This could be the last scene of the romance novel we have already written.

Now, let's make the characters more complex. In the following love scene there will be commitment but no sex. There will not even be a kiss; however, we can see an even deeper commitment between two strangers than we had in the above scene between two familiar characters. We have the elements of a love scene in that there is a bed, someone undressing, playful, sexual banter, and a whisper of devotion.

Brad entered the dingy mountain cabin where Janet sat in the tattered lounge chair he'd owned since high school. She clung to the shadows as if they were safe harbor.

"I don't have much to drink here. I don't come up here so much anymore. I've only got some champagne from last New Year's Eve."

Janet pulled up her knees and hugged them as she glanced furtively toward the door. "It'll be flat by now."

"No, I didn't have anyone to share it with."

"Oh."

Brad went to the refrigerator and withdrew the champagne, popped the cork, and poured into two mason jar glasses. He handed one to Janet, who started to drink ravenously.

"Don't you wanna toast?"

"I don't know you well enough to toast," she said.

He knelt in front of her. "I don't understand why those men ran you off the road into the icy lake. But I'm damn glad I came along when I did or you wouldn't be here."

"Thank you for saving my life."

"You're welcome, Janet. I don't know what or whom you are running from, but you're safe now. I'll help you."

"What kind of person are you? You can't save me from them. Nobody can. Nobody should."

"We can talk about it tomorrow after you get out of those cold, wet clothes. I have some flannel pajamas in the bedroom. You can wear those. There are two down comforters on the bed. You'll warm up in no time."

"What about you? Where will you sleep?"

"With you, of course," he said.

Janet jumped up. "I'm out of here."

Brad grabbed her shaking arm. "Sorry. I was just kidding."

"Bad timing."

He led her into the bedroom, gave her the pajamas, and turned down the bed while Janet changed in the bathroom. When she opened the bathroom door, the light from behind her shone through her long blonde hair. She looked like an angel in enormous flannel pajamas.

"They're too big," she said, nearly tripping on the hems as she shuffled across the floor to the bed.

"You look asleep on your feet," Brad said, holding up the covers for her.

Janet slipped between the sheets. "Thanks."

He covered her up as she closed her eyes. "Thank you . . . ."

Brad sat on the edge of the bed, watching Janet sleep. "I didn't save your life; you saved mine."

The element of the setup that makes the second passage exciting is that it underscores the deeply psychological belief in most human beings that "somewhere, out there, someone is waiting just for me." Janet and Brad have stumbled onto each other by coincidence or divine intervention. They did not plan to meet, but they did.

Brad saved Janet's life and in that we have a great "meet." We *also* have set up all manner of plot twists to come. In a few short paragraphs we have established the fact that Brad finds Janet very attractive. Obviously, even though she is terrified, she subconsciously finds Brad attractive. He made a cute remark about sleeping together and though she threatened to leave, she didn't.

This love scene hints at future love scenes between the two. The reader is already imagining Brad crawling under those two down comforters with a very willing Janet beside him.

In the above scene we have virtually all action taking place on the surface in dialogue and physical action. There is no "head action" going on.

Let's move ahead to a few days later.

Janet stumbles out of the bedroom into the main room, where Brad was sleeping on the sofa next to the dying fire. The flames flicked crimson and gold light across the walls like a painter splashes color on a canvas. She hadn't put her fear away long enough over the past forty-eight hours to really see this man who had saved her life from her husband's assassins.

Janet wondered what a simple man like Brad would think if he knew she had been married to a CIA operative and that her life had now been marked by IRA terrorists who blamed her husband for the death of one of their leaders.

Brad was just an accountant. His wife had left him because she considered him uninteresting. From the sounds of it, Janet thought his wife was a self-centered, spoiled brat and that had she been Brad, she wouldn't have hung in there for ten years with her like he did.

Janet sat on the braided rug next to the fire, where the warmth moved across her back like a cozy shawl. She reached out to move a thick lock of dark hair from his forehead. She noticed that he was bare-chested. She also noticed that his arms and shoulders were well defined and his chest was sprinkled with tufts of dark hair.

Obviously, he worked out quite a bit.

My accountant never looked this ripped, she thought to herself.

At that moment, Brad stirred and rolled onto his side, facing her, and as he did, the blanket fell away revealing a very flat stomach.

She reached down to touch his chest when suddenly she remembered herself and retracted her hand.

"What am I doing?" she whispered to herself and began to rise.

"Come back here," Brad moaned, grabbing her wrist and pulling her down on top of him.

"I should go to bed."

"Yes, you should," he said as he brought his mouth up to hers.

Janet did not pull away, and let his lips linger over hers for a long time. She memorized the feel of him and the taste of him and secretly she hoped that he was doing the same.

Common sense told her not to hope. They had only known each other two days.

His tongue rimmed the outline of her mouth and then sought her interior. She moaned.

Brad held the nape of her neck in his hand and with his left hand on the small of her back he eased her under him until he was on top and she was cradled beneath him.

His kiss grew intense. Over and over he devoured her mouth as if he'd not had any love for a long, long time. In all her life, Janet had not known passion this explosive. Though she had loved her husband, he'd never been a demonstrative man when it came to Janet. He saved his passion for his work. He had wanted to save the world.

Janet could already tell that Brad wanted to save Janet's world.

This passage has not only the action of the kiss going on, but in Janet's thoughts we discover history about her and her marriage. We hear her heart talking. We empathize with the empty, nearly icy existence she has led up until now when she has met Brad.

We have used the symbolism of the icy lake where Janet was drowning to exemplify both Brad's loveless life and Janet's loveless life. The fire in the fireplace symbolizes the passion that has been ignited between the two protagonists.

All of these elements keep the texture of our story rich and help to bring our characters to life.

NINE

Marketing within the Story

$\mathcal{T}$he American contemporary social landscape within which we all live far too often seems like a surrealistic television commercial. We have been over-marketed, over-pitched, and over-advertised. In this very book I have referred to "brand-name" authors. These authors' names are recognizable to more than just romance readers because the advertising and publicity they have been given have ratcheted them up to celebrity status.

This is all a result of expensive and targeted marketing strategy.

As a first-time writer or newly published author you need to be aware of this fact. This is your new reality as an author under a publishing house's corporate umbrella. No matter what your personality, talents, attributes, or personal characteristics, once you become a published author you are labeled and pigeonholed.

This is a good thing.

This kind of attention you and your career deserve.

However, keep these facts in mind when you are submitting your work. Do you want your precious book to come under the banner of a house that does erotic science fiction? I found a publisher that specializes in just that.

I was originally published by Avon in the late 1970s, when my fellow Avon authors and I were dubbed by the press as the "Avon Ladies." I remember radio talk show hosts poking fun and making snide, sexual innuendos and condescending jabs at me at the time. However, twenty-five years later, those same commentators and radio personalities hold the "Avon Ladies" up like goddesses.

This shows how persistence rewards itself.

When I first began writing, any reference to a brand name of any kind was instantly edited out. A "Kleenex" became a "tissue." An "Excedrin" had to be a "pain reliever." This one always makes me laugh. I remember my editor calling me from New York and saying that my character had given her eight-year-old son an aspirin. I replied to the affirmative, explaining that baby aspirin had saved my son from many a fever. We went around and around about Tylenol, calling it a non-aspirin; then we called it an "aspirin substitute;" then a "fever-reducer." This went on for ten minutes and each of her ideas sounded like a long-winded commercial. Many times the confines in which editors and authors must operate are ridiculous.

Back in those days everyone was worried about lawsuits. Then came the eighties.

Designer labels hit the mainstream in the eighties. Judith Krantz broke the barrier with her string of successful, glitzy, glamorous novels with heroines who wore Galanos gowns and carried Louis Vuitton purses.

Things in the literary world haven't been the same since.

Try to imagine television's *Sex and the City* without a mention of Jimmy Choo or Manolo Blahnik shoes. Young fashion designers get the biggest career boost possible from a mention in a novel or better still, a chance to have their clothes worn by a famous actress or model.

Let's say you are writing a period-piece love story set in New York in the 1950s. There is no way you could describe the scenes without mentioning Chevrolet cars, the Dior pencil skirts, the Shapparelli hats, Halo shampoo, or a cheap Tangee lipstick. Your heroine might drink Hires Root Beer in Chicago and a Hamm's beer in Milwaukee.

Contemporary romances almost couldn't exist without direct product mention. James Bond ordered "a vodka martini. Shaken, not stirred." Today's wealthy, traveled, and educated hero would order, "A Grey Goose martini, straight up, dirty." The brand is all-important in this line because ordinary vodka costs twenty dollars a quart, sometimes less. Grey Goose brand name costs seventy-five dollars a half gallon.

You tell a great deal about your hero in this simple line of dialogue. We now know he can afford the very best. He expects the best and will pay for it. Grey Goose vodka is satin smooth with no bite. It's not expensive just because it's a brand name. It is expensive because of the manufacturing and filtering process that goes into making the superior vodka in the world. Our hero would know this. This knowledge puts him in a class apart. It makes him special.

Now, let's dress our hero. For example, compare the two following heroes.

He swaggered only a tiny bit as he entered the room wearing a worsted-wool dark blue suit, snow-white shirt, and pale gray silk tie.

From this description we would assume our hero is a businessman or lawyer, at the very least, a professional man of some sort. He is particular enough about his appearance and the opinion of others to dress conservatively and his grooming is probably somewhat important to him.

He swaggered only a tiny bit as he entered the room, the impeccable cut to his Saville Row tailored suit revealing his very wide shoulders and trim torso.

This man has a bolder personality than the first man. Because of his athletic build, of which he is very proud, and his willingness to spend a great deal of money to dress, we could assume that he is not only an athlete, but also a well-paid one. Perhaps he is a Grand Prix racecar driver, or a famous NFL quarterback. He could even be a movie star.

As we look closer at the second man, yes, we see that he is none other than George Clooney!

I met George Clooney at the premiere of *High Fidelity* a few years ago, so I don't believe he would mind me mentioning that to you here.

In the above two paragraphs, I can guarantee I've got your attention, haven't I?

How did I do that? I mentioned the name of a famous person.

There is absolutely nothing wrong or illegal about mentioning famous people. Their names and their lives are public domain. It's what you can and cannot do with them that is the issue.

RULE #1. Never, ever cast your famous person, political figure, movie star, businessman, billionaire, or potentate in a bad light. If you can't write something nice about them, don't write it. Period. This is not to say that what you write is boring; it can be quite exciting, you just can't make them look out of character or be an active part of your story. But famous contemporary walk-ons in your story are fun and scintillating.

RULE #2. When interspersing movie stars and famous names into your story, back up your facts about them. If you are enamored with Meg Ryan and you want to use her in your story, back up your facts by reading everything you can about Meg. Do your research. Don't put words in her mouth that she wouldn't say.

Think of famous people this way: They are friends you just haven't met yet.

Boldfaced types, as famous people are termed in journalism, have hearts, lives, and feelings, too. They just happen to be famous.

If by some fluke in the universe, your book gets sold to a publisher and it becomes the biggest hit of the year and then Hollywood comes knocking on your door to buy the book rights and a producer gets your film made and in that film, he casts Meg Ryan and she decides she wants to meet you and you are flown out to Hollywood, think *now* about how you would explain yourself to her if you wrote something unkind about her.

RULE #3. If you think you'll get sued for writing something libelous, don't do it.

The same goes for products and their placement in your story. Don't cast stones. Don't use your prose as a soapbox or any other kind of diatribe. Romance just isn't the place for that kind of writing. If you truly want to lambaste a contemporary issue, do it in mainstream fiction, where voices for such writing are accepted.

This is not to say that you cannot use every variety of emotional, health, political, environmental, and social issue as your plot device or even the background. You should. Just tread lightly and stick to the real story, and that is the love story.

Marketing within a romance is a natural fit because the readership is female, and most marketing surveys will verify that when it comes to shopping, it is the woman who controls the purse strings in American households.

As a writer and especially as a novelist, once your book is published and read, your readers take your words quite seriously. You can be of special help to other struggling artists, painters, designers, fashion designers, or entrepreneurs by putting your friends or contacts in your stories.

I've written several novels based in Texas over the years. While I lived in Houston, I was involved in many community and charity affairs as well as fundraisers at various times. I was asked early on by a particular sculptor if

I would mention his work in one of my novels. I saw the man's bronzes and was quite taken with his work. He did not have a name at the time and was struggling, and so, I agreed to give him a mention.

In my story, I had the heroine, Hailey Asher, working in an art gallery after her divorce. She is enamored with the work of a sculptor and though the artist is not a character in the story, his work is something that is featured in the gallery.

Years after this book came out, I was at a charity auction and was approached by this sculptor. He told me that by mentioning his work his sales had increased considerably and a large gallery in New York had asked to see his work. I am not by any stretch of the imagination taking any credit for his success. He was very, very talented. What I did do was give him exposure. He, in turn, gave me exposure by mentioning me, my book, and my subsequent novels to his friends and clients.

This kind of networking is imperative as the years go on and you write your second and third and fiftieth novels. The products you mention today in your story might seem innocuous, just part of the story, but as time goes on and your work becomes more well known, those products may be the very companies that a film producer might approach for funding for the film version of your story.

As in everything there is a pitfall to avoid with name-brand product placement within a story. It's so easy to reach overkill status.

Let me demonstrate.

Channing slipped into her Victoria's Secret tap pants and camisole, slathered her legs with Boucheron body lotion, and then wiggled between the Ralph Lauren sheets.

We can see her, smell the perfume, and know the sheets are expensive. However, we've used three brand names in one sentence. We have a vivid picture of the scene; however, our goal here was to create a sensual mood. Let's revert to using our ace in the hole—our imaginations.

Channing slathered her long legs with a creamy apricot-scented French body lotion Brad had bought at the duty-free shop in Amsterdam. She slipped into a pair of midnight blue satin pajamas with white piping on the lapels and cuffs and then, ever so quietly, she snuggled under the down comforter and spooned herself next to Brad.

I'll place my bets that Brad is not sleeping, wouldn't you?

This scene is far more sensual and yet we haven't mentioned a single brand name. Now, let's ramp it up and give it some punch in the proper manner with some brand name usage and see what happens.

Channing slathered her hips with Shalimar scented body lotion, taking her time, knowing that Brad was not yet asleep. Pulling the down comforter away from his chin, Brad leaned over to the dresser and picked up the rolled black-satin spaghetti strap of Channing's favorite Victoria's Secret merry widow. "I'll get the garter belt, if you get the stockings."

This scene is not only visual and sensual, it's fun. There is no question about what is going to follow for this couple. In this last example, we see that Channing is a sentimental girl, having chosen expensive Shalimar, which is a nearly one-hundred-year-old scent, founded in Paris. The choice of this perfume reveals that she likes romantic things, things and people that last. She might even be quite conservative in her everyday life, but at night, she thinks of herself as both romantic and a vixen.

The merry widow, or corset, is already lying out on the dresser. She wants Brad to see it. She is playing a game with him to keep the romance alive and exciting. Brad is adorable as well. He's been watching her dress for bed.

Channing puts the lotion on her hips, not her calves. The author could take time here and describe, either graphically or humorously, Channing's particular application of the lotion to her hips. Maybe she sings a song while she's smoothing the lotion into her skin. Maybe she gyrates her hips for Brad. Maybe she walks around the room, going behind a wing chair, into the bathroom and back just to make him a little bit nuts.

All these elements are fun to play with when creating your scene.

It is always wise to keep product placement in mind when writing, but always bear in mind that a little goes a long way. Choose your products wisely and they will be the glitter you need to give ordinary passages sparkle.

TEN

Query Letters, Synopses, and Submission Packages

You have spent the better part of one year writing your book. You have had your family, friends, and even strangers in your writing group critique your work and help you with your novel. You have lost sleep over this project, but finally, there comes a time when you must let it go.

You must (gulp!) send your work to the agent or, in some cases, the publisher.

When you are finally ready to submit your work, this is the time to be your professional best. You want to make a great first impression.

Because the romance genre is so broad and encompasses so many sub-genres, you must be very specific to your chosen sub-genre.

Romance publishers and agents are inundated with query letters and submissions every week. The more you do your homework for your submission, the more likely you are to sell your work.

This book has reiterated the importance of choosing a sub-genre. In your query letter you *must* state your chosen sub-genre and the name of the publisher's line to which you wish to submit. In no other genre of fiction is this point more vital than in romance.

Therefore, if you are submitting to Harlequin's Intrigue or to Silhouette's Desire lines, you must state this in your letter.

Having kept those publisher guidelines in front of you while you wrote every day will now prove to be extremely valuable.

The subject of the query letter and its vital importance in the process of submission has long sent chills of revulsion and fear through many an author. In workshops and lectures at writing conventions you will hear editors and agents expounding upon the necessity of perfecting the query letter. Beginning authors shake in their boots over the prospect that after all their long hours of work writing their book, now this one single-page letter could annihilate their dream of getting published. This fear is so real that there are query letter classes and workshops all across our country.

In most instances you will be submitting your query letter to an agent, not to the publisher. The truth is that there are less than a handful of publishers who still accept un-agented submissions.

There is no hard-and-fast rule about the timing of your submission, but as a beginning writer it would be best for you to have completed the entire book. If the agent were to be intrigued by your query letter and answered you back, wanting to see the book immediately, you would be the one slowing the process down if you had not started the book or only had fifty pages written. For a beginning writer there is a great deal about writing that you are going to learn between the pages of fifty-one and four hundred and fifty-one.

There are instances of new authors "feeling out" the marketplace before sitting down to the computer, by querying agents and then going forward once they have received a response. You may hear these stories at conventions and the results were successful. If you choose to go this route, then by all means do so. Do what feels natural and good to you.

For the most part, however, it is always best to have written the book or at least a very large part of the novel.

You should know your word count when you submit. You would not want to submit a 70,000-word-count category type of novel to MIRA for their 125,000-word-count contemporary line. This is another reason to have finished and rewritten your book several times so that you reveal your intelligence and your "homework" by knowing exactly the publisher's criteria for the line to which you are submitting your work.

Query Letters

The query letter is a single-page letter in which you introduce yourself and pitch your novel to an agent or a publisher.

There is a skill to writing an interesting query letter and it's not all that difficult.

Be clear.

Be concise.

Hook them.

To accomplish the above, follow these guidelines:

1. State your name and make sure you have your return address, e-mail, and phone number in the letterhead. Believe it or not, there are people who have missed this step. How can the publisher or agent get back to you if you don't provide all your information?

2. You need a "hook" line of description that sums up the story.

3. Provide an overview of the story in as concise a manner as possible.

4. Provide your writing background or credentials or if none, education and a brief résumé.

These points must be covered in your query letter.

Tips for Writing a Winning Query Letter

The Overview

Here you will mention the exact sub-genre of your novel.

If your book is a contemporary romance, that's fine, but give it more definition. Is it paranormal? Romantic suspense? Romantic thriller? Chick-lit?

For your first novel, please try *not* to call your romance "mainstream." Too many beginning authors believe that their novel is somehow "more important," "more literary," or "more prestigious" if they call it "mainstream." The fact of the matter is, too many times, your novel is not clearly defined in story. Sometimes, not always, the plot is not developed properly, which translates to: *boring*.

You can begin to see again why it is so very important from the day you start plotting your story and building your characterizations, that you fit your story into one of the publisher's sub-genres.

If your romance still does not fall into a sub-genre, and you are dealing with contemporary women's issues within the plot and characterization, then it is "women's fiction."

If there are no social/political/moral issues involved, and no humor, but it involves a family history or interplay between family members, then it is a "family saga."

Do not make the mistake of mentioning that your book is a historical and leave it at that. In this case you must mention if it is a Western, Scottish, Medieval, etc. If your story's location spans more than one country, mention those exotic locations to give your overview information a bit more flair.

Example Overview

"My completed manuscript, *My Spanish Heart*, is a 100,000-word historical romance."

The above overview sentence gives us a lot of information, but it could be a lot better and give even more details.

"Set against the backdrop of the glittering capitals of Europe to the beaches of Andalusia, my completed 100,000-word, eighteenth-century novel of romantic suspense, *My Spanish Heart*, is geared for the Harlequin Historicals or Avon Historical Romance lines."

In this overview sentence we have given the following information:

1. The fact that the book is completed.

2. The word count.

3. The fact that this is a historical romantic suspense.

4. The publisher's lines to which the author wishes to submit.

5. The specific guidelines the author followed in the writing of the novel.

These last two points are very important in today's market. When you consider that an editor is reading upwards of one hundred or more query letters a month, you need to be very specific in the information that you give to the editor.

If you want your book to be submitted to Harlequin's Steeple Hill Chick Lit/Mom Lit, then state that fact here in the overview. Once you have stated this fact, then you will need to state that since your book is 98,000 words, it fits the criteria of Steeple Hill's guidelines of 80,000–125,000-word count. This shows the agent and publisher that you have done your homework. You are aware of all the guidelines of the line to which you are writing.

FYI

Most editors still go by the 250-word-count per-page system. This system has been around for decades and means that the author is using Courier New font, 12 point, with twenty-five lines per page and margins no smaller than one inch and no larger than one-and-one-quarter inches.

The Hook

This one-sentence description of your book should be snappy, unique, and in the best possible manner display some of your writing "voice."

Some writers can get it all into a single sentence, but if your hook requires two or three short sentences, don't become unglued over it. The point is to entice that agent/editor to want to read more.

Sample Hook Lines

"Sparks fly and comets collide when astronomers Lacy Lane and Gil Griffith battle theories and their attraction to each other, in a race to obtain federal grants."

"Steamy tropical Miami nights have never been so electric as when Janie Tamblin, night court justice, must pass sentence on Rick Barrows, arrested for a gas station robbery and who vehemently proclaims his innocence, though all Janie sees are the searingly sexual looks Rick gives her."

"Romantic illusions turn into life-threatening nightmares when Ali Simon buys a haunted house from sexy realtor Jake Callaway."

Each of these lines contains a brief description of the story and they leave the reader wanting more. When devising your hook sentence, practice springing the line on friends and family. If they respond with interest, that's a good indicator of what you can expect from the agents and editors.

If this kind of writing is still too difficult for you, go to the bookstore and head to the romance section. Read the blurb on the front of the cover of those published books. The copy editors who write these captions and blurbs are as good as it gets. Read the back cover to get more ideas. The more you familiarize yourself with some of the "zing" words of the genre, the better your query letter will be.

Check out your cable guides for those short listings of television movies of the week or feature films. Look at *TV Guide*. Watch the movie posters in the theaters and read their blurbs. Another good source is the newspaper on Friday when all the ads for the new film premieres are advertised.

Your hook sentence for your query letter is advertising. Plain and simple.

If you can come up with a hot log line, the rest of your query letter will be a snap.

The Hook Paragraph

There are just times when your story is too long to be condensed into a single sentence. Don't fret. A very concise paragraph will still work. It is best to have a "hook" sentence, but if you don't, your life's work is not going to be flushed down the tubes.

The following is a blurb paragraph on a book I'm writing, called *Wedding Belle* for chick-lit.

"Overweight Belle Matthews is about to inherit her grandfather's millions so long as she marries before her twenty-sixth birthday, which is only one month away. Desperate to keep her fortune, she bargains with her former high-school chemistry partner, Jeff Sladick, to become her husband for one year, and in exchange, she will pay for his medical-school tuition after a quickie divorce. Jeff agrees, never suspecting that Belle has withheld a vital piece of information . . . she must produce an heir within the first eighteen months of marriage."

Writing Credentials/Résumé

Now that you've sold your book and your story, you have to sell yourself.

This information should be about your writing affiliations, awards, how many books you have finished, and other writing such as articles for magazines or newspapers. If you can say it succinctly or if it is pertinent to the book, mention your education.

If you just wrote a romantic legal thriller and you are an attorney, you should state this.

If you are a working astrologist and this background was part of the futuristic romance you just wrote, you would also mention this.

You would not mention that you have two children, one husband, three dogs, and a cat and that due to this family structure you feel you are an expert on family life for this romantic family saga you just wrote.

Query Letter Don'ts

1. Don't take up the editor or agent's time with tidbits about your family life or extemporaneous hobbies of yours that have no bearing on the story.

2. Don't tell the editor that you spent a decade on your book. Editors are looking for writers who are prolific and can produce a book a year.

3. Don't tell the editor that you have a disease and that this gave you the inspiration to write something before you die. Again, publishers want their writers healthy and happy.

4. Don't misrepresent your novel in your query letter.

5. Don't try to fit your book into what you think the agent wants to hear.

6. Don't send the letter in with typos.

7. Don't forget to thank the editor or agent for taking the time to read your query letter.

8. Don't send the query letter via singing telegram or some other "attention-getting" marketing trick. Editors know good writing when they see it. If your work is good, no amount of flowers or chocolates is going to sway her one way or the other. After the editor has bought your book and she has worked with you, you should thank her often for her hard work. Send her the chocolates for her birthday and send her flowers at Christmas.

9. Don't fail to have someone else read and re-read your query letter for you. The chances are you are so nervous about sending out your book, you will not see or properly read what is right in front of you. Two pairs of eyes and two brains here are absolutely better than one.

10. Don't forget to include a stamped, self-addressed envelope and a stamped self-addressed postcard with your query letter. This is so that the agent or editor can write you back.

One Last Tip

At some place in the body of your letter you should mention if you are only submitting to this particular agent or editor. If you are sending multiple query letters out, then state that clearly.

Multiple Submissions

What should I do? you ask.

Frankly, agents and editors are split on this issue and always have been. After nearly thirty years of being an author, I have to say that the best advice again, is do what feels natural to you.

If you feel comfortable sending multiple submissions to agents, I would suggest to pick the top three you like. Perhaps you've gone to conferences and met a few agents. Perhaps the friends you have in a romance writing circle or a chapter of Romance Writers of America have recommended their agent. If you have any kind of personal relationship with an agent, nurture it.

Send out one query letter to that agent and wait for his/her response.

If you have no connection to a writer's group or have never been to a romance convention, and the only list you have is the one found in the writers' *Guide to Literary Agents*, then you might feel very comfortable sending multiple letters to these strangers. In this case I would send no more than five letters out at one time. Wait for the responses and see what happens.

I have talked to first-time authors who start at ten or even twelve agents at one time. This is a lot of folks to keep track of, but everyone has their own style.

If you have the good fortune to have a friend or acquaintance who is an author and they will recommend you to their agent, you are a blessed person. Do everything you can to cultivate this relationship.

If this agent gets your letter and sends it back to you and states she is not interested, don't stop there! You've got your foot in the door and if you take your foot out, it's your own fault you aren't published.

Write her back or e-mail her and ask her very, very politely, if it was your story or if the houses she represents simply have "filled their list." This means that no matter how good your story is right now, this agent's contacts in publishing aren't buying.

Then and only then, if you get a response and she says it is your story, ask if you can schedule a phone conference with her and talk to her for only ten minutes. And then stick to the ten minutes!

Agents are always impressed with writers who really mean business. If you didn't hit the mark with this story that does not mean that you can't write another book. If you can prove to this agent that you are going to keep writing no matter what, and that you will change your existing manuscript in any way necessary to make it be the marketable story you know it deserves to be, that agent will never forget you.

Authors don't get sold with perfect manuscripts. Editors are always improving on our books. Don't think that your rejection letter is the result of a really bad book. Maybe it's damaged, or was never whole to start with, but that doesn't mean you can't fix it. Fixing it is all the fun!

Once you have your ten-minute conference call with the agent, take her advice to heart. Make sure you wrote down as many points that she/he told you about your manuscript.

Tell the agent you are going to make these changes immediately. Thank her/him for all their time and expertise. Tell the agent you will get the changes to them in less than six months. If you give yourself a year, it's too long.

Agents want to see commitment.

Your book is finished. You have something to work from. Now, throw your ego out the window and hunker down and do the work.

Call the agent when the work is done and ask if you can resubmit the novel to her. She will be happy to see how her input influenced your revisions. If you've done all she asked, your chances of having an agent represent you are as strong as they can get.

Pat yourself on the back. You have done the construction work of building your own dreams.

The Waiting Game

Most submissions to agents and editors are going to take at least six weeks. Sometimes they take longer. The waiting can be nerve-racking. Try to avoid the temptation to call the agent or editor.

If you have not heard anything after six weeks, send a postcard, a note on nice stationery, or a typewritten letter inquiring only if your submission letter was received. There is always the chance that it got lost in the mail. It does happen.

All agencies and publishers log in submissions. They are given numbers, dates, and all kinds of reference. If your letter did not arrive, they will know it.

In three months if you have not heard anything from the agent, send a note or postcard again. Usually by this time, you will get a response of some kind.

While you are waiting, do not be idle. This is the best time to start plotting your next novel so that when the agent calls and says, "Yes, I want to represent you. What else do you have?" You will be ready with a new story line to pitch.

The above sample query letter covers all the bases that we have discussed in this chapter. Please note that our "hook" line is the second sentence of the paragraph in which we give the brief story line. The hook sentence does not have to be the very first sentence in your very brief synopses but it should be either first or second, as a general rule.

Double-Check

Before you send your query letter off, pick up the phone and call the agent's office to which you are sending the letter. Spend the money for this call because you want to find out if the agent is *still working there*. You will have wasted valuable time if the person you seek now lives in a great house in Tuscany.

Ask the assistant on the phone to give you the correct spelling of the agent's name and double-check the complete address.

This may seem like a waste of time right now, but think how awful it would be to waste months sitting by the phone that is never going to ring because the person you seek is no longer with the agency.

Sample Query Letter

Your Name
Street Address (Apt. #)
City, State, Zip Code
Telephone/Cell Number/Fax/E-mail

August 11, 2004
Ms. Nancy Albright
Romance Authors' Agency
1000 Times Square
Suite 1200
New York, New York 10019

Dear Ms. Albright:

My completed manuscript, *Rescuing Roxanne*, is an 80,000-word contemporary chick-lit romance, which I wrote for Silhouette Bombshells.

Marina del Rey is the playground of Hollywood moguls and starlets. Roxanne Wilson, a deputy sheriff who patrols the waterways for drug traffickers and smuggled aliens, saves a drowning film director, Lance Adams, from certain death and discovers that it is her heart that needed rescuing. Roxanne's handsome and sexy boss, Jim McGrady, does not believe Lance's near-death act and thinks that Lance is directing a multimillion-dollar shipment of cocaine into Los Angeles. Roxanne sets out to prove her boss wrong and at the same time keep Lance very, very close, hoping to learn the truth behind a series of waterfront drug-related murders. Risking her heart and her reputation, Roxanne is just about to unravel the mystery and discovers which of the two men in her life is worth rescuing, when she realizes that the truth will be the cause of her own death.

I have been writing for three years and have completed a romantic suspense and a Western historical. I hold a Bachelor of Arts degree in English and am a member of Lambda Iota Tau, national literary fraternity. I have worked as a features editor for a local neighborhood newspaper for the past seven years and have published several articles in national magazines, including *Cowboys and Indians*.

I look forward to your response and I have the completed manuscript of *Rescuing Roxanne* ready to submit upon your request. I have enclosed a SASE for your convenience. I can also be reached by e-mail at audra@author.com or at 333-333-3333.

Should you wish to learn more about me, including viewing my headshot, I have a new Web site: *www.audraauthor.com*.

Thank you very much for taking time to consider my work.

Sincerely,

Audra Author

If the assistant tells you that the agent (or editor if it is a publishing house) is no longer working there, ask for the name of another agent or editor who is now handling romances for them. Then get the name of the assistant and write it down. Thank her for her time.

The next time you call the agency, ask for the same assistant and call her by name.

Even if you never work with this agency again, that assistant could become an agent, and ten years from now, she just may remember your professionalism and courtesy. She may be your agent in the future.

Synopses

After you have a positive response from the agent or the editor, you may be asked to submit a synopsis. Agents are very busy people and they do not usually read full manuscripts. Therefore, the synopsis takes on great importance since this is the first writing the agent will see.

Why a synopsis and not the manuscript? You will need a synopsis to submit to your agent if you do not have your manuscript finished. If you have jumped the gun and sent out queries prior to finishing the book and the agent is "hot" to see more from you (we hope!), then she/he will ask for the synopsis while you are finishing your book.

You will need a synopsis for some agents and editors even if you have your manuscript finished, because some agents don't have the time to read the entire book. Many times, agents will know that a particular house is "buying" at that particular time. The agent has fallen in love with your query letter, and from the sounds of your fabulously written "hook" sentence, she/he thinks they have a very good shot at getting your book sold. Remember, the agent works on commission. They need product to sell. The agent also knows that certain publishers will buy a book with only a synopsis and a few sample chapters, even from a first-time author.

What is a Synopsis?

The synopsis is a short version of your entire novel.

Depending upon the line to which you wish to submit and for which you are writing, the length will vary from twenty-five pages for an 80,000-word manuscript to more than sixty pages for a 125,000-word manuscript. Judge the length of your synopsis by how long you believe your novel will be. Thus, if you are writing a six-hundred-page historical with intricate subplots and a multitude of characters, you will do yourself a disservice if the synopsis is only twenty-five pages long.

As with the manuscript itself, the synopsis should be double-spaced on one side of the paper and unbound.

The Romance Synopsis Is Different from Other Genre Novels

Most genre books—mysteries, science fiction, horror, and the like—are plot-driven books. Great attention to the plot and how it unfolds must be represented in the synopsis.

Romance synopses are different in that the emphasis must be about the characters. Your goal is to make the agent or editor fall in love with your heroine and hero.

You will need to include as much detail as possible about the characters. If you choose to fully disclose the backstory on the heroine, do so. There are no hard-and-fast rules in this area, but giving the backstory does not hurt your efforts.

Any kind of detail that you believe will bring out your heroine's character is essential.

If you so choose, write some sample dialogue that gives real insight into your heroine.

Write scenes with as much action and dialogue as you can at this point, even if you haven't written the book. These passages will draw the reader into the synopsis so that they get a real feeling for your story.

Imagine that you are an editor reading your fiftieth synopsis for the month. Try to think like the editor thinks: She's looking for a special "spark," a special "voice" that she either hasn't seen before or is reminiscent of a famous romance author who writes for another publisher.

She's overworked. She's harried and yet, she's got a Friday night at home when there is nothing on television and she's just made a cup of latte tea.

What would she want to read?

She'd want to be taken into a world that is very different than hers. She's read just about every romance plotline in the book. BUT she has never read your heroine. She has never heard your voice.

This is your chance to dazzle her. You do that by painting your story with character-specific details. When your heroine speaks, her words should reveal something about the heroine's personality. Using dialogue to explain entrances and exits, affirmations of action that has just been described, or to expound upon the background and setting are a waste of your time and your editor's time.

Use dialogue to reveal your heroine's thoughts and emotions.

Use dialogue to reveal the conflict/attraction between the heroine and the hero.

You will not be using a great deal of dialogue in the synopsis; therefore it must be truly revealing and well placed.

Placing Dialogue Within the Synopsis

Your first two pages of the synopsis should be utilized to set the background, setting, and explain the backstory of the heroine or hero, if necessary. The setup of the plot should be stated.

Once you have introduced the hero and the heroine, you may choose to show a scene by using dialogue.

In the middle section of the story, in which the plot becomes more complicated, use dialogue during the explanation of the breakup scene. The agent/edi-

Sidebar: Exceptions

There are instances when all of the information we have discussed above is not appropriate for your situation.

Face-to-Face Meetings with Agents or Editors

Because the romance field is so very active with networking, and publishers supporting workshops, writer's conventions and the like, you may meet your chosen agent face to face, which eliminates the necessity for the query letter.

Let's say you are at a party, convention, workshop, seminar, or in the airport, and you meet—ta da! A real literary agent. If you have been formerly introduced, such as you would at a seminar in which everyone knows his or her roles, the agent is open to what you have to say.

If you meet an agent in a public place by coincidence, this is not the time to talk to her about your book. The agent is pitched stories and projects at every turn of her life. However, you should never slide over an opportunity. If this is the case, explain that you have written a book or that you are writing a book. Tell the agent that you absolutely will not destroy his/her evening, afternoon, trip, etc., by going into details. However, you are a professional person. *Ask for the agent's card*. Tell the agent you will send her/him a "package." THEN GO AWAY.

tor will want to hear your characters' voices during this time. Use the dialogue to reveal the innermost thoughts of the hero and heroine.

In the end section, use a bit more dialogue in your scene descriptions. Dialogue will help move the reader quickly to the conclusion.

The Complete Submission Package

Generally, after the agent has responded to your query letter, the agent or editor will dictate to you whether he/she requires the synopsis and three sample chapters or the entire manuscript.

Take your direction from the agent and do exactly as she or he requests. DO NOT DEVIATE FROM THEIR INSTRUCTIONS.

You will need to write a cover letter in addition to the synopsis and chapters, or the entire manuscript.

Sometimes you will have an agent request the synopsis and the entire manuscript. Again, do exactly what the editor or agent requests.

The complete submission package should include:

- ❧ *A cover letter*. The cover letter should be no more than three or four lines. Include your address and all your contact information. Thank them again for taking the time to peruse your work. Tell them that you look forward to hearing from them. Only mention the title of the book; don't pitch the book here as you would in a query letter. Know in your own mind that you are beyond that point. You have a relationship with this person now.

- ❧ *The synopsis*. Make sure the pages are not wrinkled, coffee stained, or bound. They should be paginated, double-spaced, and on a single side of the paper.

- ❧ *Three sample chapters*.

These should be the first three chapters in the book and ideally, should be somewhere between thirty-five and fifty pages. Any agent or editor can tell if they are "hooked" into your story by these first three chapters. If they are not, you have some rewriting to do.

- ❧ *A résumé or bio on yourself*.

This should be a single page. State your education background, awards or honorariums you have received for your education such as summa cum laude, etc. List your writing achievements, awards, or any other pertinent information about your writing career, as you would have done in your query letter.

❀ *Include a photograph that looks like you.*

This is not imperative, but I have heard this tip from editors who go to huge Romance Writer's of America conferences or the Maui Writer's Conference or the *Romantic Times* Writer's Conference. They have stated that they meet hundreds of beginning authors and it is difficult to keep everyone straight. Even when they remember a particular story or pitch, they may not remember the name. By providing your photograph, you help them familiarize themselves with the story, the name, and the writer.

In the situation we are discussing, when you have met an agent or editor, the query letter you wrote is out the window. Don't send it.

You have met the agent face to face. Perhaps the agent actually asked a bit about your story that you pitched to her in your one-sentence "hook" line you spent all those hours devising.

Your synopsis and the first three chapters of the story should be everything the agent needs to read.

Again, only in the circumstance that you met this agent, it is a good idea to include your photograph to help him/her remember who you are. *If you have never met the agent, then no photograph is necessary.*

If you have a résumé including your education, writing awards, or writing background, include it.

The wise person would be as professional as possible when putting this submission package together.

Mailing Instructions

If the agent has requested your material, place everything in a FedEx box or envelope or a Priority Mail box or envelope. Do not use a battered old box covered with cut-up brown paper grocery bags.

Double-check to make sure your cover letter is in the package. If you have a business card, include that.

On the outside of the box or envelope, in the large white space, write *"REQUESTED MATERIALS."*

Submission Don'ts

❧ Don't include CDs or floppies of the manuscript.

❧ Don't send your cousin Louie's mock-up of what you think the cover art should be.

❧ Don't send a handful of computer-generated bookmarks advertising the book you have not yet sold.

❧ Don't forget to thank the agent/editor for reading your work.

Working with an Agent

If you peruse the Romance Writers of America's Web site and you look under "Market Update," where the publishers list twice a year what they are looking for, you will see most often, "No unsolicited materials accepted."

This means you have to have an agent to submit your work.

This is the twenty-first century. You have to have an agent.

Do you understand? You have to have an agent.

Agents generally charge 10 to 15 percent of the total advance you are given for your book. They get the same percentage on all your royalties in perpetuity. Because most romances go on the shelf and off the shelves within a few years, most times that agent is not going to be making money on you for the rest of your life. Unless you are Nora Roberts or Judith McNaught. Their books are still on the shelves twenty years later.

Why would you want to pay someone 10 percent or 15 percent of your money?

Agents not only are just about the only conduit in the publishing world between you and a sold manuscript; they can save you hundreds, even thousands of dollars due to their familiarity with the various publishing houses' contracts. You would be amazed at the convoluted, one-sided terminology in publishing contracts that exist to make a very large corporate conglomerate even richer. "The devil is in the details" must have been written about publishing contracts.

A good agent who has been around for awhile has taken many publishers to task over those pesky little details. The agent knows from experience what buttons they can push and when.

Once you understand the *value* of an agent, you will respect that person, and from that basis, you will enjoy a solid working relationship.

If you start out your working relationship with someone you don't respect or whom you believe is cheating you, you will get divorced.

Just as every relationship is different, so are author/agent working partnerships.

This is a business relationship. The agent is not your girlfriend or best buddy who has time to hear your tales of woe.

Be as professional in all your dealings with your agent, because you know you are going to be around for a long time providing good projects for your agent to sell.

Rules for a Respectful Relationship

1. Understand you are important to your agent, but you are not all-important.

2. Your ego is a quality you should park at the door. No one likes a prima donna.

3. Once you hire your agent, provide him/her with all the materials he/she requests.

4. Ask the agent if they prefer that you contact them through e-mail or via the phone.

5. Never call an agent on a Monday. Mondays are too busy in New York for any human to survive!

6. When possible ask via e-mail if you can set up a phone conference with your agent so that you have her/his undivided attention.

7. When speaking with your agent, have a list of items you wish to discuss and stick to the list.

8. In general, all of publishing moves slower than it did even five years ago. There are fewer people sharing the workload. This includes your agent. He/she can't work miracles. He/She must work within the confines of the editors' schedules and the idiosyncrasies of the publishing world.

9. If you have a problem or true concern, call your agent and explain to the assistant in detail what the problem is. The assistant can relay that message to the agent and you will get faster attention.

10. Always thank your agent for the time they are spending with you.

Finding an Agent Who's Right for You

Finding the right agent for a beginning writer is nearly as difficult as it is to write the book. Agents are overwhelmed with work and the good ones have a client list as long as your arm of writers who are making them money.

However, every year, dozens of agents go to the writer's conferences we have mentioned numerous times in this book, but they bear repeating: The Romance Writers of America Convention, usually held in July of every year, the *Romantic Times* Convention, the Maui Writer's Convention, and the various chapters of Romance Writers of America's chapter conventions or workshops.

Literary agents and their agencies are listed in several publications each year. These guides are always on the shelves and in the computers at your local library.

A key source for finding an agent is to go to the romance section in your bookstore. Most romance authors dedicate their books or have honorable mentions, which will include their agents, managers, and favorite editors. Make a list of these agents. When you go home, on your computer, run a Google search for the agent's name. Once you have the name of the agency or agent, you can find the appropriate contact information you seek through several of the search engines.

To contact the agent, pick up the phone. When you get the agency on the line, ask the receptionist if the agent you seek has an assistant. If so, talk to the assistant. If not, ask the phone receptionist if they know whether or not your chosen agent is accepting new clients. Some agencies are literally closed to new writers. These agencies represent the Danielle Steeles of the world, and they don't want an author until they have been published a dozen times. These are the Tiffany's of agencies. Very few of us will walk their hallowed halls.

Once you discover that the agent is still accepting query letters, send your fabulous query letter that day! Don't put it off. After all this detective work, get the ball rolling.

AAR?

All agents are not licensed or regulated in some jurisdictions. The Association of Authors' Representatives has standards and procedures that its members must uphold. However, not all agents doing business as literary agents are licensed. You must ask the agent if they are licensed or at least make the answer to this question part of your homework before you even call the agent.

Help from Published Authors

If you are blessed enough to know or meet a published author at a workshop or seminar, it is absolutely fair to ask the name of their agent.

If you get to know a published author for more than a nanosecond, then you can ask if they recommend their agent. These are two different questions.

Litigation in our world today has cut off a valuable source of help from the established author who once helped a beginning author. Very, very few published authors can or will accept your synopsis or manuscript to read and recommend. The situation is rife with possible lawsuits.

Do not ever send a manuscript to an author without his or her express permission. The only thing that will happen in this case is that it will go in the trash. Published authors don't have time to read your work and they certainly don't want to risk a lawsuit.

Save the submissions for the licensed agent.

Signing with an Agent

As a beginning author you may be asked to sign a contract with your agent.

Always have your attorney read this document. You don't have to have an attorney read your publishing contract; that's what you have the agent for. But you should have an attorney read and advise you on the agent's contract.

There are a few bad apples in every barrel, right? It's no different for agents. Therefore, make sure you know what you are signing.

Accepted Practices

Agents' fees vary, as we have stated earlier, from 10 to 15 percent of your income. Some agents charge as much as 25 percent. If the agent is asking for a larger sum than 15 percent, make certain this agent is providing extra services that are not part of the standard agent's duties. These extra services could include procuring publicity or media press coverage for you. It could be the arranging of a book tour, speaking engagements, and even representation for film and television projects based on your books.

None of the above listed services are provided in a standard agreement for a literary agent.

You also need to check the section of the contract that pertains to foreign rights and fees. Some agents take as much as 30 percent if they are the agent of record making the foreign sale. If you sell your book to a large publisher, that publisher will initiate and conduct the foreign rights sale. Then your agent should only be taking their standard 10–15 percent. If your contract does not state this, negotiate this item.

Don't agree to "expenses." If your agent demands expenses, frankly, they should be no more than a hundred dollars every quarter. There should be no possibility that your agent's plane trip to London next month will show up on your billing.

You should have an out-clause in your contract, giving you the ability to get out of your contract by simply writing a letter to your agent, and within a thirty-day period thereafter, you are both free to go your own way.

When the publisher pays you the advance and the royalties, the money will go to the agent. The agent will deduct their fees and then send you the balance. This is traditional within the publishing industry. The agent should not retain your money any longer than two weeks. I have heard some authors scream over this two-week "holding period." For most of us, we just factor that time period into our personal budgeting considerations.

It's another story if the agent holds the money for longer than that or has overlooked your royalty check. If you are expecting a check and it has not arrived, do not hesitate to call the agent and ask about the check's whereabouts. When it comes to money, agents are always willing to pick up the phone and talk. Money makes them smile. That's why we hire them.

Most agent contracts are not complicated and fairly straightforward.

What an Agent Will and Will *Not* Do for You

Your agent should agree to represent ALL of your work. In the publishing world this would entail your current book and the next book after that and so on.

Working without an Agent Contract

Some agents have no contract at all. Basically, you are doing business on a handshake. This is not uncommon and, in fact, if you have a relationship like this, whether it is to your advantage or not is a constant source of debate in the publishing industry.

Most times, having the written contract allows the parties to know exactly what the parameters of the relationship are. There are no questions.

When the agreement is oral, later in the future, when everyone (especially you) is not so excited about the fact that someone loved your book, you may not remember that the agent said she expected you to pay her phone bill every month.

One of the pitfalls to an exclusive written agreement with an agent for a certain period of time, like two years, is that if the agent doesn't return your calls, or doesn't want to give you that strategy session she promised you, or fails to get the advance she had promised you she would, and you are feeling very disappointed, you are stuck for those two years.

With a handshake agreement, if you have concerns, you can move on. If your agent is not performing for you in any way, you have the ability to move forward with your career and hire another agent.

If you want to get out of the relationship, phone the agent and explain why you want to move on to another agent or work by yourself.

Hopefully, this scenario will not happen to you. The only reason you would want to break relations with an agent is because they have not performed for you, breached a contract, or you have discovered something nefarious the agent has done. These situations were very, very rare twenty years ago, but sadly, all of us are hearing such stories today.

Working without an Agent

It is possible to work without an agent, but in today's very competitive romance market it will be difficult. You will only be able to submit your book to a handful of prominent publishing houses. However, there are dozens of small independent publishers who do not pay advances and are looking for romances.

You will spend a great deal more of your time on your business than on your writing.

If you work without an agent, you will absolutely need to hire an intellectual property attorney to read your contract. A word of advice: A standard contracts attorney will not understand a single word of a publishing contract. Publishing contracts are incredibly one-sided to the publisher's advantage. To deal with this kind of business is not the same as if you were selling widgets. Get a good attorney who has experience with the publishing world.

NOTE: Foreign rights are usually divided between the author and the publisher, fifty-fifty. Your contract may be even more explicit, with royalties on each book sale stated in percentages. With some globally distributed publishing houses, their foreign royalties are typically 4 1/2 to 6 percent of the cover price of the book sold in the listed foreign markets. You can negotiate these percentages, but don't expect the rates to be too much higher. A general rule of thumb is that the foreign rights percentages will be roughly half of the domestic royalty rate.

Make no mistake—foreign sales are more important today than they have ever been. As I stated in previous chapters, film revenues in the global market have risen a great deal to the point that the majority of gross revenue for American films now comes from foreign markets. The same is true for American books.

To be even more precise, some publishers have gone after foreign sales with aggression. These publishers will continue to have rising sales figures in the future and that is what you should be concerned about—your future with your new publishing house.

Contacting an Editor Directly

You have decided to go solo on this writing career of yours and now you want to find just the right editor to whom you will submit your work.

1. Go online to the Romance Writers of America Web site and find "Market Update." There you will find a listing of the names of the editors associated with every line or imprint within each house. You will also discover if those editors are accepting unagented material.

2. On the same Web site find out when and where the next writers' convention is taking place and, if possible, make arrangements to go to the conference. If you can't afford this conference, see if there is another Romance Writers chapter near you that you could join.

3. Write or e-mail the editor to whom you wish to speak and try to set up a face-to-face meeting with the editor at the convention. Chances are the editor will ask for a query letter or even a submission of your synopsis prior to the convention so that she can advise you once you do meet. If the editor knows you will take pains and spend the money and time to travel a long distance to meet her, she/he will make an appointment with you.

Choosing a Publishing House

When you began writing your romance you chose the criteria and publisher's guidelines that best suited your novel. In your way at that time, you began pre-selecting the editor and the house you would write for.

Whether crassly commercial or literary, you may admire the way one house markets their authors, as opposed to another house. All this should be taken into consideration when you think of where you would like to place your book. I would advise you to consider this as well while you are writing the book. If it means altering your writing style to please a certain publisher, there is nothing wrong with that. You are just starting out. You are in the process of finding your writing style. My style has evolved dramatically since my first book. If it hadn't, I probably wouldn't be published today.

Self-Publishing

Some romance authors get very discouraged in the pursuit of finding a publisher and opt to self-publish or vanity publish. In this instance you would be paying for the book to be printed.

Sidebar: Handling Rejection

Part of the writer's life and career is rejection. Sometimes I wonder if all writers aren't masochistic, because if you haven't been banged around enough by life, being a writer and getting rejected will surely add a little drama to the mix.

I know this sounds patronizing, but don't take it personally. I have discussed this somewhat in this book in previous chapters, but dealing with rejection slips and letters can be handled in two ways.

The first one is childish. Keep your ego inflated and blame the editors or agents. You can call them names, think they are idiots, and scream, yell, and run around in frantic circles and pretty much throw a temper tantrum.

Or you can gather up the letters and compare the comments made in each one. Is there a common theme running through them?

It used to be that editors would give you a very valuable paragraph about what was wrong with the story and why they didn't like it.

These days my rejection letters (yes, I still get them) offer me little insight into what is going on in the mind of the editor who reads my material.

If the letter is very short and offers no clues, you can draw the conclusion that the publishing house probably had other books by already-published authors to fill that slot.

I term this the "Civil War Syndrome." Remember how I pointed out that books about the Civil War don't sell? They don't. Also, many houses have a writer they've worked with for decades, and if that writer loves to write about Ireland and your book is set in Ireland, chances are they will reject your story on those criteria alone.

However, after you've gone over the letters, and if you find even two letters that say something similar or the same thing, such as "I didn't care for the heroine," then bingo! That's your answer.

To fight the depression you are feeling from this rejection, the best defense is a great offense.

Immediately, pick up your manuscript and read the story with your editor's viewpoint that everything seems to be okay, but she didn't like the heroine.

Believe it or not, sometimes it is just the dialogue that needs to be changed. Maybe she's too petulant. Maybe she's an idiot. It could be that she gets herself into dumb situations and gets out by even dumber logic. Make your heroine smarter. Make her more sympathetic. Editors want to read heroines they can identify with and with whom they believe the readers will "fall in love."

Understand that this route does not guarantee or even promise that the book will be distributed.

After you have your book printed, you will buy X number of copies and they will sit in your garage until you sell them on the street corner.

Only respected independent presses and large publishers, after years of forming relationships, make their way into the "system" at Barnes & Noble or the wholesale distribution of Ingram Books and the like.

If you are still having problems getting published, look to the manuscript, not to the publisher.

Publishers are buying romances all the time. If your novel still misses the mark, don't give up. Your timing may be bad. You may need to rewrite.

The best advice is to write another book. Then another book if you have to. Most published authors have a book or two in finished manuscript that is sitting on a shelf that just "missed the mark."

Vanity publishing is fine for psychologists and public speakers who are going to sell their book in the back of the room. Romance authors don't have an audience like that. They must rely on retailers to sell their product.

You could lose a great deal of money by vanity publishing. Most publishers in this area will charge five thousand or more dollars to edit, set, and print your book. Art and graphic costs can run that up to ten thousand.

If you have this kind of money to spend, then go to the library again and in the Literary Market Place reports issued every year, you will find a list of vanity publishers.

Most cities have private presses who will print books for a fee.

There are some independent publishers who will co-venture with you. That is, they are already a part of the Ingram system and can at least get you into the wholesale "machine" even if there are no retail outlets promised. Such publishers will ask for five to seven thousand dollars from you to pay for the first print run.

Again, in the romance field, this is not advisable for the future of your career. The romance-publishing world, as a whole, does not consider this to be "published." It has taken years for Internet publishers to garner recognition for their e-published romances. It's a tough road. But then, you are a romance writer and you believe in happy endings, right?

ELEVEN

The Publishing Process, Editors, and Authors

*P*ublishing companies are in the business of selling books. Their corporate efforts are spent in the pursuit of profits.

Romance publishing is a very profitable business. The competition for romance is more intense than any other genre because there is a huge market for the books, as well as thousands of aspiring writers who want to be published.

As an aspiring author, you have a dream. You put the dream on paper.

The publisher's dream is to make their stockholders happy. They do that by selling large quantities of books.

The above is not meant to patronize you in the least, but you would be astonished at how many beginning writers just don't "get" that publishing is a business. They think that the literary world is philanthropy. It's not. The publisher doesn't care that you've dreamed all your life of being published. They care if your book makes them money. Publishing is a business.

Once you reach the hallowed halls of a publishing house and begin to work with an editor, your life has just entered a new dimension.

Thus, it is understandable that as you are just beginning your writing experience with your romance story you want to tell you may or may not have given consideration to the world of publishing. Publishing is as vast and varied as there are countries around the globe. It's hard enough, you say to finish your novel, much less expand your mind to all the considerations that are going to be made about your book.

This is just the time for you to educate yourself on what the ramifications and advantages are to understanding the publishing process. If you have an insight into the process your book will go through in order to be published, you may then better understand much of the business and marketing information discussed in this book.

Remember when we addressed the simple notion of where you want to see your book? That very fact will have a direct impact upon the publisher's decision of where and how to market your book.

In this chapter we will address this and many other aspects of the purchase and the sale of your romance.

Understanding the Publishing Process

You have been successful in acquiring an agent, who sent your book to a dozen publishing houses. Happy Romance Publishers has an editor who has fallen in love with your book. Your agent tells you that your book is going "to the committee" or "to the board" for consideration.

You have no idea what this means. What's going on behind those doors? And is the consideration for a romance any different than for a mystery?

Committee Criteria for Acceptance

The question here is, who has the power to make the decision to buy your book?

1. The Editor. In order for your book to even "get to the table," the editor has to go to her superiors and pitch for you. She has to believe not only that your book is good writing, but also that you can do it again . . . and again. Perhaps she has two backup synopses, just a few pages of story ideas, for two more romances from you.

2. Market Trends. The editor has called the publishing company's in-house sales reps or contacted their sales department and inquired if your racy, spicy, contemporary romance is selling well in the marketplace. That phone call or contact has more to do with your manuscript getting picked up than most authors would like to imagine. If the feedback is positive, the book will move on to the next phase of acceptance.

3. The Board. Every publishing house has a board or committee to which the editor presents your story. She will pitch them based on the work and the fact that your book is similar to best-selling author Suzy Q and that their publishing house needs an author like you because they have no racy, spicy, contemporary romance in their line. The editor will then present your manuscript or synopsis and first three chapters to the board to read. The committee, then, depending on the house, read your work before they all convene again and give their approval.

NOTE: This process could take six months, but the average is anywhere from one to three months. If your book was submitted in the summer months, many editors take a much earned and necessary vacation, which will slow the process.

4. Review Standard Contract. Once the committee or board approves your novel, the editor will send their standard contract to the agent. As a first-time author, you don't have much negotiating power for this contract. Again, this is why having an agent is so very important to you. There are items in the contract she may want to "push" for you, and they aren't always just an increase in the advance. Sometimes, you may want to take a smaller advance (such as, in the event your genre is really a hot seller and this publishing house has nothing like you and the book was incredibly well written; your agent may push for larger royalty percentages and larger foreign rights split).

5. Contract. Your contract is finalized.

6. Editor's Note. At this stage you will receive your editor's changes and notes to the manuscript, and you will be given a certain amount of time in which to make these changes to the manuscript. You will have one to two months (generally) to make these changes. We will address these issues later in this chapter, as well.

7. Acceptance of Manuscript. Your manuscript is accepted. Your book will now go to the copy editor and there will be changes, usually miniscule; factual information will be required; sentence revisions; typos. You will be given a certain time period to get these changes done—usually two to three weeks.

8. Book to Print. Now the book goes to graphics, print set, and the art department will finalize all their plans for the cover. As a beginning author, you will probably not have any say or decision in the cover art. Don't put any expectations on your cover. The art department works with marketing and they know just what sells. You don't. You know how you would like to see the cover, but leave the professional decisions to the professionals. Whatever you do, don't complain about the cover if you don't like it.

9. Galleys. Galleys will be printed and sent to reviewers for review. Sometimes reader's copies will be sent to the big chain buyers and to the sales reps in your publisher's company. This is not always the case with beginning authors, but many houses do this. If the sales reps like the book and actually read it, they will recommend your story during their sales meetings with the buyers. Most times, the reps only get a few blurbs, but if your story is like best-selling romance author Suzy Q, they may remember her latest book and recommend your story because it is similar to Suzy Q's. This is precisely the action the publisher is hoping will take place when they send a reader's copy to the sales' rep.

10. Publishing Dates. Your pub date could be set at any time during the publishing process. Sometimes the book is put on the publisher's schedule at the time of the contract. However, this date could be rescheduled once or twice, especially for new romance authors. As a general rule, most romance houses always have a "new kid on the block" and they don't move those new kids around, but it does happen. The publisher has a huge financial and time investment in you. If they discover that Suzy Q's racy, spicy, contemporary romance is coming out the same month as yours, they may move you to give you a chance to be read.

This is good for you. Romance readers are not going to buy two of the same genre in the same month. They may buy one western historical, one category romance, one best-sellers-list romance, and one unknown author every month. But that last-place position, which is where you are with your first book, cannot compete with Suzy Q when she writes on the same subject.

11. Marketing and Advertising. A book's promotion budget is a direct reflection of the big chain's order. If the buyers at Barnes & Noble, Borders, Books-a-Million, and the like place large orders for your book, the publisher will be likely to invest in a book tour of some kind. This could range from in-store promotions in your local area to a nationwide tour.

Remember when we discussed the setting of your story having an impact on your sales? This is where that comes in. If your story is set in Texas, the chains and your publisher's sales reps will push your book in that area only. You may get in-store signings. Another real boost to sales are the cardboard holders called "dumps" that you see in the local chain stores. Your publisher may pay extra to have your book featured in the front of the store on one of those tall rolling carts you probably have seen.

End caps for romance have always helped boost sales. The publisher has to pay for these end caps.

A broader canvas for the story, such as a car chase story line I chose in *California Moon*, which encompasses Louisiana, Texas, New Mexico, Arizona, Mexico, and the Mediterranean, then the publisher will push for larger, nationwide distribution and marketing. The publisher would then consider a national co-op ad campaign in which the publisher and distributor split advertising costs. We will discuss this in depth later in the book.

12. The book is out. The first time you see your book on a bookstore shelf you should be covered with chills and near to tears. If you aren't, remember, this is the moment you worked for. This is it! Very few authors will make it to the best-seller lists with their first book. Becoming a best-seller is a goal we all aspire to and it takes years and many books to make it.

Don't ever be discouraged about anything you encounter during the publishing process. Remember that it is a process. Your writing is a work in progress. Also, remember that while the publisher is going through all its steps to get your book out to the public and make money on your title, you should be fast at work on the next book you want to submit.

Inside the Author/Editor Relationship

In my estimation, *editors are angels.* I believe that if you look closely, they have wings and can walk through walls. Look even closer and you will not be able to figure out how they do all that they do. Editors today are incredibly overworked due to a great deal of consolidating on the corporate level. Between staff meetings, appointments with agents, conferences with fellow editors, meetings with sales and marketing departments, and long trips to writers' conventions there is very little time for them to do what they actually truly love doing the most: working with the writers.

Couple all that with the fact that all editors have "slush" piles in the corners of their offices—slush piles that just may hold a real treasure of a book. These editors are dying to read through the stacks of submissions to find that gem, but it's no surprise that they don't have time—in fact, how can any of them have a personal life at all?

In the beginning of my career, I had about four or five editors and assistants who worked on my book. All kinds of folks got their chance to kick around my not-very-well-written book. Except for a few editorial assistants who were still in high school or who were working for a temp agency the day my first drafts came in, most of my association with editors can be summed up as an exceptional postgraduate degree in both writing and publishing. I know what I know thanks to the brilliant professional men and women who have guided my publishing career. However, for them and for me, none of it was easy.

My personal learning curve, if graphed out, would look like the "Hell's Ride" roller coaster at a theme park. This is because I interspersed my early career by writing one historical suspense, then a contemporary romance, then an action/adventure, then a murder mystery historical, and then a family saga. You get the idea. I was an editor's nightmare.

I had an editor who asked me why I did this. "Why can't you just simply write the same book over and over? Everyone else does."

My answer: "I'd get bored."

That was back in the days when romance as we know it now was trying to figure out what it was, too. Editors jumped all over the place trying to find what was "hot." One year they claimed historicals were "in," but only the ones set in Scotland, and thank you, but their list was already filled with enough Scottish lassies. The following year they wanted steamy contemporary novels.

Working on my IBM Selectric, I couldn't write fast enough for all these supposed "market trends" and still hold down my regular weekly job.

Then, publishers, editors, and their boards of directors got smart.

The truth is, if it's romance, it's all hot.

For those of you who are new to the romance genre, the canvas for you is limitless. Ten years ago half the sub-genres we have in romance didn't exist. Many of the "rules" according to each house were nowhere near as broad as they are now.

Editors welcome all sorts of new perspectives to our genre and they are open to listen as never before.

The world of publishing is fascinating and ever changing. Your editor is more than the writing partnership you have foreseen. She is the key to world-wide acceptance for your book.

Making the Relationship Work

Once you have an editor and your book has been accepted for publication, work with your editor as much as she asks. If you have met your editor at one of the Romance Writers of America conferences, such as we discussed in the last chapter, you already have a hands-on grasp of that person's personality.

If the editor was crisp and to the point with you on most subjects, and if she seemed pressed for time at the convention, chances are her work schedule back in New York will be much the same. Thus, when you contact her via e-mail or on a telephone call, make your statements and questions clear and to the point. Don't be telling her about your cat's latest adventure.

If, on the other hand, your editor met you for lunch and perhaps had read your book prior to the convention, then you would have a different relationship with her. The editor might have wanted to know YOUR personality. She might have asked a great many questions about your life and your family and barely touched on your book at all. If this is the case, it's a good indication she is looking for a long-time working relationship with you.

One of the excellent aspects of the Harlequin/Silhouette corporate structure is that once you are acquired by an editor and she (usually) becomes your champion, that editor is the same editor who will guide your career throughout your tenure with their company, no matter which line you want to write for. This keeps the relationship very special.

Many published authors will tell you that they have had experiences in which their editor's mind and their own thoughts were so in sync that someone listening from the outside would think you both were psychic. Just as a husband and wife, or two very, very close girlfriends seem to be "on the same wave-length," when you are doing such intensive work as writing a novel, this would be the best of all situations.

That kind of relationship can come about when you spend the time and energy to adapt your schedule and manner of doing things to that of the editor.

You are just beginning your career in publishing. The editor has been there for years. Most of the senior editors have been in their positions for as long or longer than most of the brand-name best-selling romance authors have been writing. That's three decades. That's a lot of knowledge and experience they have. Keep this in mind when you think you have a grievance or gripe.

So, please, if you are lucky, and many of you will be, if that synopsis of yours is strong and your first three chapters are engaging, and if your book is accepted before you write the manuscript, your editor will call you and confer with you about the story. When she tells you that she would like to see some "structural changes" made, don't panic, and please, don't take this as a combative situation. She is there to make your story better.

Here are some basic rules for building a good working relationship with your editor:

Rule 1: Accept that All Books Can Be Improved

Trust me, there is no story ever told that still could not use improvement. Every author has at least one book they would love to rewrite, even with the glowing reviews they received years ago.

If this is your first novel, there will be a great deal that needs work. Be ready for it, and then you will not find your spirits deflated when your editor tells you that your second favorite character in the book has to be eliminated.

Rule 2: Know When to Stand Your Ground

Always discuss your most heartfelt positions with your editor. Let's say your editor loves the entire story but she wants to change the hero substantially. Instead of a sweet guy in the beginning, she wants him to be a rebel. Don't recoil.

Instead, ask your editor why she wants this dramatic kind of change. If your editor gives you valid, logical, and pragmatic reasons for the change, then open your eyes and make the change. I have had to do this in the past, and at the time, I thought my editors must surely be certifiable.

The experience of altering your main character into a person he or she was never intended to be when you set out to write the book will teach you volumes about writing, rewriting, and will push the envelope of your creativity to new levels.

During this process, you will teach yourself how to be totally objective. Without that kind of objectivity that your editor has, flaws in your writing, in your story, and in your character will eventually disrupt the entirety of your novel.

Sometimes there are passages that you believe add a certain "voice" to your writing. If you truly believe that this passage should not be cut, make out a list of all the reasons why you want to keep it. You should know precisely how this passage, plot point, or scene enhances the main characters or advances the ultimate plot. Be as clear as possible. If you can, point to references later in the story that hark back to this scene.

Then call the editor and discuss this with them. If you show that you have very valid reasons for keeping in the story those points or scenes that you value, usually your editor will understand your viewpoint and allow the passage to stay.

Rule 3: Know When to Compromise

If your book is flawed, it will be either in the characterization of your hero or heroine or in the plot.

Editors have very strong ideas about what will make your heroine more memorable and more individualistic. Most times with a new author, that editor is going to be telling you to "show" not "tell" the aspects of your heroine. This will mean translating that flamboyant prose you spent hours devising into action and/or dialogue scenes that best reveal your heroine or hero to be proactive. When it comes to helping you make the heroine stronger, heed the editor's advice.

When you are writing your novel, you know your heroine inside and out. She comes to you in dreams, talks to you, and wants you to tell her story on paper.

Your heroine is your best friend. You believe you have portrayed her perfectly.

However, your editor is saying that the heroine isn't "coming through" in a clear, interesting manner. Take the cues your editor has given you in her cover letter or in the margins of the manuscript.

Spend some time thinking about the direction she is leading you and then do the work. Once you start rewriting you will see how much better your characters are.

REMEMBER: The editor has already bought your book. She championed for you with her board or committee. She believes in your work. All the editor is trying to do is make your characters sharper and more memorable to the readers.

The second area you will address with the editor is that of plot. Most beginning authors have a basic plot down pat, but there are "windows" or "chances" in the story line in which the plot could be more complex and the story made richer.

Let's say you killed off one of the supporting characters, a male, early on. Your editor wants you to keep him alive so that later in the story he becomes attracted to the heroine, even to the point of proposing to the heroine. This gives the heroine a dilemma, a choice to make, and reveals through her actions how deep her love for the hero is when she rejects the other suitor.

The plot could be made even more complex if this supporting character could not emotionally handle the heroine's rejection. His mind flips to the dark side. He threatens the heroine. He stalks her. He tries to kill the hero.

Now your plot is even more expansive.

Why is the editor doing this to your perfectly sweet romance? Because this plot sells more copies of the book.

As we stated at the start of this chapter, the publisher is in the business of making money. They will guide you to write stories that will continue to sell many copies of books.

Rule 4: Always Remain Professional

Once you learn, through the help of your editor, how to read your own writing with your editor's eyes and mind, you will have learned what it is to be a "professional writer." Professional writers can write nearly on demand. They are the kinds of authors who publish at least once a year, if not six or seven. A professional writer does not "agonize" over a revamped plot or the insertion of a new subplot or the elimination of a clunky character. The professional writer takes the advice of her editor and analyzes it, and unless there is some major flaw in the editor's view, the majority of the time the editor is always right.

There are some published authors who are going to faint over that last paragraph. Their "pride of authorship," their ego, is so strong, so distorted that they believe that whatever they write is golden. Personally, I believe the day you find yourself buying into that kind of thinking is the day your creativity shrivels up and blows away.

Rule 5: Remember Writing Is a Team Sport

Writing, whether on a novel or a screenplay or teleplay, is a joint effort. Yes, the book is yours. But there is a great deal of collaboration that goes into the finished product that hits the retail shelves and the best-seller lists.

I don't have any personal success without the help of so many people behind the scenes, it's hard to count them all; but I know who they are and I will never forget them.

In my early college literature classes, I studied Maxwell Perkins's biography. Maxwell was the editor for F. Scott Fitzgerald. I remember this particular book being a collection of letters from Fitzgerald to Maxwell. It was amazing how much extra work after the first draft of each of Fitzgerald's books Maxwell demanded. There were letters of praise and near-adoration from Fitzgerald to his editor. I always remembered those letters each time I sat down to go over my editor's notes on my latest novel.

If you will keep in mind that even the literary legends had editors who forced their young protégés—and make no mistake, that's what beginning authors are—to alter their stories, enhance their dialogue with precise vocabulary specific to the character, and to rewrite until it was perfection.

Remember always that your editor is pooped! Send her a thank-you note, especially when you think she's out of her mind for wanting to cut the cute baby scene you've labored over for weeks. She deserves a pat on the back and so much more.

How to Deal with the Emotional Highs and Lows

I don't care who you are or at what point your writing career is right now; when an editor or critic reviews your work and finds it wanting, it hurts! You wouldn't be human if you didn't respond with tears, depression, anger, and even the occasional physical violence of throwing your manuscript at the wall.

It takes a lot of determination to rein in your emotions and plunk your bottom back in your desk chair and go to work slicing up your hard work, not to mention as much as a year or more of your life.

For my first two or three novels, when my editor sent me my list of changes and editorial notes, I remember curling up in a ball and crying like a baby. Four hours later, I would pull myself together and promise myself that after this, I would never write again. Yeah, right.

Once I'd drowned my sorrows in a couple brownies, two scoops of vanilla ice cream, and hot fudge, I would start reading the letter again. Then, again.

I found that after about the sixth pass of the editor's letter, I would start making my own notes. Then I would compare those notes to the manuscript.

By attacking the work, I found that my creative juices were flowing more than they had when I originally wrote the book. Even slight nuances of direction would bend my mind and force it into a new and better direction.

It was at this point that my mind switched, like a train track switching lanes, from writer's head to editor's head. Suddenly, I could see my characters with keener insight. I started analyzing my own plot from my editor's point of view.

You are not alone, nor are you the first writer who has ever reacted emotionally when they've received their editor's edit changes.

It is absolutely normal to get even a little depressed at this time. After all, your publisher liked the book enough to buy it, right? They told you they thought you were a fantastic writer, that you had an unusual point of view or the freshest voice in fiction in the last decade.

Then you get a four-page letter, single-spaced with all the changes that if you did make them, your new novel would bear little resemblance to what you originally wrote.

Been there, done that!

Remember all those months of research to accurately describe the interior of a whaling ship on which your heroine stowed away? You spent fifty bucks on discount research books, hours on the Internet, and even took a tour of a whaling ship in Boston to really get the "feel" of the vessel. Now your editor wants her to travel by land in a stagecoach instead of by boat, "because we already have a story about a girl on a ship coming out the month before your book."

Right about now, your world is spinning out of control. You'd tear your hair out, but there's none left after you finished the grueling last chapter of the book . . . on time, we might add.

Emotionally, this book has been rougher on you than going through nine months of hormonal hell before the birth of your first child. That goes for fathers as well as mothers.

And here I am, telling you that this editor's letter is the best thing that could ever happen to your writing.

Several times in this book I have discussed what it takes to be a "professional writer." That professional mind-set must at all times take into account the marketplace. That includes your publisher's schedule and that of their competition.

Hollywood does this all the time. They shoot a film, only to find out that Studio B is doing a film on exactly the same subject at the same time. Therefore, they hold the film back for release, sometimes for years. It is not uncommon for the film never to be released to theaters at all. Consider the frustration, anger, and disappointment of the screenwriter in this situation as well. Every writer looks to the release of his or her work as being a career stepping-stone to the next book, the next success.

If you do not allow for a wide leeway in your own thinking and in your emotional response to events as they unfold, you will drive yourself crazy and you will begin to abhor the writing process. I have always believed that knowledge and information are the keys to awareness. If you know about the pitfalls of your writing career from the outset, you can prepare yourself for the disappointments so that when an alteration in publishing dates affects your book and your life, you don't take it personally and you don't run through the streets screaming. The best thing to do at times like this is sit down and write another book, knowing that your first book is going to be so much in demand that publishers will be knocking on your door asking, "So, Miss Smith, what *else* do you have?"

In the final analysis, I believe that nine times out of ten, my editors' ideas were brilliant. This is not to say that I always acquiesced to every editor's whim, because I didn't.

Use what you learn from one editorial session to apply to the next novel you write. Eventually, you will find yourself honing your skills through your editor's efforts. Frankly, she is hoping this will happen. This is how a publishing house "builds" an author. Your next novel should go more smoothly. Less editing. Less work on both your part and that of your editor. If you pay attention to what she shows you on the first book, your second writing experience will be more fun and less painful.

TWELVE

Self-Promotion (or Please Don't Wear that Antebellum Costume to the Book Fair)

*P*lease understand that at no time in your writing career will self-promotion cease to be important. It is critical to your continued success. Without promotion, your numbers just aren't going to grow.

The climate in just about every aspect of the business world has changed so much in the past five years to include self-promotion. Salesmen have always known that to get the job done, you have to sell yourself first. The customer has to like you first, and then they will take a look at your product.

When you go to a restaurant and are met with a surly person at the front desk who is seating folks, the chances are that if you don't like their attitude, you'll walk out. The same is true with any kind of retail establishment.

As I've said, books are business.

Publishers are selling a product.

You are selling yourself to the publisher just as much as you are selling your book or your idea to the publisher.

A few years ago, I had a nonfiction book I was pushing around New York and other places. Because I was a romance novelist, I was in very uncharted waters for me. There were no familiar acquisition editors to talk to. My agent didn't handle nonfiction very much and really didn't want to spend valuable time taking me to a "new market." Therefore, the job of selling the book fell on my shoulders. What a learning experience this was.

One of the publishers I talked to liked the book concept and thought there was a reasonable chance that the book would sell. Still, the editor wanted to talk to my agent first, even though I'd made the initial contact. At the time, I didn't think much of it. I called my agent at the time, and the agent said, "Sure, I'll call them."

When the agent called me back I asked if there was a problem with the book. The agent told me that the publisher rather liked the idea and knew that I could write the book, but that wasn't the problem. The problem was that the publisher wanted to know what I looked like, and my agent had faxed over a headshot.

I was stunned. I wasn't an actor. I was a writer, after all!

Yep. The publisher was already thinking about publicity and promotion.

How will she look on camera? Does she do public speaking? If so, is she any good? How does she handle large groups? Is she better suited to small groups and small towns for her book signings? Can she sell the book in the back of the room? Will she tour? How does she handle book signings? Can she do a city a day? More than a city a day? Will she get national talk shows? What large newspapers have ever written anything about her? Has she been on national television news shows? Any national profile programs on her??

Again, in my life the angels had blessed me because I had done all this kind of promotion and more. I didn't start out on *The Montel Williams Show*, though I finally got there.

You can do the same thing.

Building a Grassroots Publicity Campaign

When my first book, *Bound by Love*, came out in 1980, I had no idea what I was doing. I was too dumb and ignorant to know that there was a right way and a wrong way to handle my own publicity. Heck, I barely knew how to write, much less how to promote.

This is the time for you to go back to your childhood and think of a time when you either acted in a school play, interviewed someone for your school newspaper, or spoke in front of your classmates in your speech class.

As rudimentary as they are, these are the same skills you will need to hone to promote your book.

When I was a young girl, I used to visit my Uncle Dick, who was a local radio announcer. A few times he actually let me say something on the air.

That experience helped me to become fairly well versed during radio interviews when promoting my book. I at least knew what a radio station was. I was not frightened about the microphone because I simply pretended that my loving Uncle Dick was there to help me.

When *Bound by Love* was published, I remembered that warm feeling of being in the radio station soundproof room. At the time, I didn't know anyone else who had published a book and so I figured, this was a fairly unusual thing to have happen to anyone.

I went to the Houston phone book and made a list of every single radio station in town and I started calling them. I didn't have an agent. I didn't have a publicist. I just had chutzpah.

I hadn't even written a formal pitch. What I did have was a glowing review from *Publishers Weekly*. I surmised that was ammunition enough. And it was.

Over a two-month period I booked myself on more than thirty local and area radio shows. Some were at four in the morning and at midnight. Back then, I had to physically go to all the stations. Live phoners weren't done that much in those days. In a way, it was terrific because I gave a signed book to the DJ or talk show host and then I took an extra copy for them to give away on the air.

One of the radio show hosts doubled as a television weatherman. He was pretty impressed with a local resident (even though Houston was the fourth largest city in the United States, they think of themselves as a small town) making it into the big bad mean world of New York publishing. He got me an interview on the local morning television show prior to *The Today Show*.

Nobody had videotape machines back then, but the studio gave me a beta tape of my interview. I used that tape to get a couple more very obscure cable television shows with a viewership of less than ten people, I'm sure.

However, none of that mattered. What I got out of it was *practice*. In my estimation there is no such thing as too much exposure to the media or too much practice. If you are lucky enough to get a television show, count your blessings. Those shots are golden; I don't care if it's one minute in between the news and weather reports.

The same is true of radio. Just keep calling stations in your immediate area until you get a show. You can ask each station manager about the size of their listening audience and this will help as well if you are restricted on the amount of time you can spend in your week for promotion. This is especially difficult if you are holding down a day job, as I was at the time.

The thing that saved me is that radio shows are often before dawn, or later at night. Perfect. I could go to a show before work or schedule one after work.

Undoubtedly, the radio station will ask you for a press kit or information package.

Sidebar: Hiring a Publicist

For most first-time authors, hiring a publicist is an expensive move. There is no guarantee that the publicist will be effective in helping you to get media gigs. Most publicists traditionally have charged a monthly fee that ranges anywhere from fifteen hundred to five thousand dollars. For this fee they will work for two to six months prior to your book coming out.

Approximately six to nine months before your pub date, you will want to make the decision to hire a publicist. You will need a few months to find the right person for you.

Where to Find a Publicist.

According to Jodee Blanco's invaluable book, *The Complete Guide to Book Publicity*, there are two kinds of publicists: freelance and PR firms.

The freelance publicist works from his/her home or in your home or the publisher's office. They tend to have very few clients. They work on a book project for only three to four months. They generally charge by the hour, a flat rate fee for the entire project or they will charge a monthly fee plus expenses.

Some will be listed in the phone book, but most of them advertise themselves by word of mouth. This is the kind of publicist you will discover through one of your fellow members at your Romance Writers of America local chapter. Ask everyone in your chapter if they know of local freelance publicists you could use. For a first-time author, you do not want to spend money on a publicist in Los Angeles when you live in Des Moines for the reason that almost all the publicity you will be able to garner for a first book is going to be "local."

If you know any published authors you have met at a workshop, convention, or seminar who have used a publicist, ask if they would share the name of their freelancer.

PR firms are definitely listed in the phone book. Again, ask other authors whom they have used in the past or if they know of a PR firm that specializes in book publicity.

PR firms are more comprehensive than a freelancer and cover a broad spectrum. Not only will they handle and book your book tour, but they also will consult on marketing, advertising, and promotions or "events." PR firms usually charge a monthly fee plus expenses. Some will charge a flat fee.

For a PR firm it is not unusual for their flat-rate fee to cost thirty thousand dollars or more.

Most first-time authors are looking for a three-week or one-month publicity "blitz" and don't require a PR firm which would focus on advertising and promoting you over a much longer period of time.

Services Provided

Let's say you have decided on a freelance publicist. Even though the publicist is going to work for three months, it is a wise idea to begin to shop for your publicist six to nine months prior to your pub date. If possible, settle on more than one person and interview two to three people.

The Interview

1. Your first question should be to ask the publicist what famous authors they have represented. Are any of them romance authors?

    NOTE: It is very, very difficult for a romance author to get television or radio dates because romance is considered by the media to be impossible to publicize.

    Ms. Blanco and myself totally disagree, which we will discuss.

    As a general guideline, the publicist will give you a few former clients to call for references. Seldom is the circumstance that the publicist would not do this.

Talk to the client. Tell that client (who may be famous or rich) that you are a first-time author. If you know what your print-run is going to be (we will discuss this later), then explain that to the client. There are times when a very famous author will give you advice based upon their own finances and their million-copy print runs. Always keep this in mind during the interview.

2. How long have they been a publicist? Look for someone who has been around the block for a decade, either on his or her own, with another PR firm or formerly with a publishing house.

3. What is their track record? What shows have they been successful in booking and for whom?

4. What are their contacts? They don't have to get you on Oprah, but they should get you a good spot in the local and surrounding newspapers, some cable shows, and possibly national affiliate television. They should have contacts in all the major cities of the state which you live.

5. Is the publicist creative? Can they come up with some ideas for your specific campaign? Do they know the questions to ask YOU to understand your goals and your beliefs? There is more here than just booking media. It must be the right media. You should have a clear picture in your head of how you see yourself and your work being promoted. Do you want to be described as a "hot and racy" romance author when your story is geared for the Christian market?

6. Ask to see some of the press kits they have designed.

7. Ask about their current client list. Is it long? Is this person overwhelmed and stressed out? How can they fit you into their schedule if they don't have an assistant?

8. How do they charge and bill the author?

Publicist Billing

As we stated, freelancers and PR firms bill slightly similar to each other.

The monthly fee is a flat rate charged each month for the period of time you and the publicist have agreed that you will work together.

The tricky territory is when the publicist starts talking about EXPENSES. This refers to the expenses they incur for getting you and your book into newspaper print, magazine articles, television interviews, and radio shows. *These expenses can run into the thousands.*

You or your publisher will need to provide copies of the book, press kits, and headshots. All this costs money. The publicist may or may not provide slick folders for the press kit materials. Are you going to pay for these?

Most times, the publicist sends the press kits and the books via FedEx. If that publicist sends out one hundred press kits at a FedEx fee of thirty dollars a pop, you will be liable for three thousand dollars in expenses. There is a reason for this. The radio producer or television producer on the other end of the line has a short attention span. They get "pitched" a dozen times a day. If your materials are not on their desk the next morning, even though they are "hot" after the publicist has successfully pitched you, they will forget you. There are circumstances when Priority Mail—which is only four to eight dollars for the average author press kit and book—will work. These will generally be with local area radio and television programs, but not national talk shows.

Ask the publicist about long-distance charges and other printing charges such as color copies of your cover, which can cost a dollar or more a copy.

The Contract

Ask the publicist to put everything in writing and get a contract. Very few publicists will work without a contract because there is a lot of room for misunderstandings in the "media game." Those misunderstandings result from the times when there are no results.

No publicist can guarantee even the first booking for you. That doesn't mean that they didn't put in the time and work. It means that if there was a national or natural disaster and all the television media decided to focus on that current news story, your tiny three-minute "gig" on the local news channel probably won't get booked or could be cancelled.

In addition, no publicist can control what an interviewer is going to ask you or how that interview is going to be slanted. Even though the publicist landed you a prime-time segment on a national affiliate television channel, there is no guarantee that the "spin" will hold you in a good light.

Six Months Prior to Release

The only reason you would want to hire a publicist this far in advance is if the publicist has *strong* magazine and newspaper connections. Most magazines need submissions six to nine months in advance of when the magazine would come out.

For you, that would be the release date of your book. Magazines are interested in either excerpts or feature articles in regard to authors. As a first-time author this would be hard to get unless your publisher paid you a sizable advance for your book and you have some strong indication that your reviews are already going to be excellent. Your publisher or agent may have told you that there is a "buzz" about your book. This would be an indication to think about, but not necessarily to hire a publicist this early on.

Two to Three Months Prior to Release

If you are working with a freelancer, this is the time when the publicist is going to be doing the bulk of the phone calling and pitching. On a weekly basis you should call the publicist and ask how it is going or at least e-mail them for an update.

If your publisher did not get you a few book signings in your local area, your publicist can get this accomplished.

Though it sounds like an easy thing to do, the chain bookstores have altered the landscape of book signings. The community relations rep (CRR) in each of the chains must get permission from the corporate office to allow you to sign books in their store. Some publicists go right to the corporate office and set up several signings. Some ask the individual CRR for a booking. Once the CRR knows you have hired a publicist, you have a very strong chance of getting the signing.

In the larger cities now, the big chains like Barnes & Noble will not allow more than one signing within a certain mileage area. Thus you could get one signing in St. Paul and one in Minneapolis. Then you would branch out and do one Borders, etc.

If the publicist is doing their job, six weeks prior to the book's release you should have several bookings for media—either radio interviews or television spots, hopefully, prior to each of the book signings you have scheduled.

A Final Word

Some publicists will not take romance authors as clients. They say this because they aren't all that creative. It takes a bit more work to push you and your romance book, but it can be done.

The Nonfiction Spin

I learned a great deal about promotion and publicity in the eight-plus years that I worked with Jodee Blanco as my publicist. Paramount in publicity for a romance author is to give the author and her book a nonfiction spin.

Every author has a "message" they want to convey through their romances. In my case it was *The Evolving Woman*. In my novels, I threw so much tragedy at my heroines to test their strength that I became known for this.

Therefore, Jodee deduced that my nonfiction spin was the fact that I was adamantly concerned with domestic abuse.

For twenty years, I worked in my local area to raise awareness for domestic abuse and how to stop it.

We devised a nationwide contest in which women who had lived through domestic violence, had gotten out, and had triumphed with their lives would write a five-hundred-word essay and submit it to Jodee's office. Jodee arranged a free weekend spa trip for the winner.

Television and radio producers loved it. They booked me on shows with other experts or alone to discuss domestic violence. While on the show the announcer would mention my newest novel. Thus, there was no discussion about the romance—only about my "cause célèbre."

The entries came across the fax by the dozens, then the hundreds. We had no idea we had hit a visceral chord in America, and it was not good. (Every six seconds a woman in America is physically abused by her husband, lover, or partner.)

For years we collected the stories, put them together, and with the blessing of HCI, the *Chicken Soup for the Soul* publisher, they printed the book.

This story is important because it can help to illustrate how you can work with your publicist to find that nonfiction spin that can help you publicize your book. Interestingly, once you do, you may discover areas of your life, and your impact on the lives of others, that you had no idea existed.

Charity

All of us have a special charity we support. Let's say yours is animals. You have donated money to the local SPCA. Your romance features golden retrievers in the story.

If you were to donate a portion of your royalties to the local SPCA, you would have a "local news interest." Local radio stations and television stations would be more willing to put you on a talk show to discuss the particular problem your community is having with overpopulation of dogs and cats or animal abuse.

The publicist could put together a television "show" on which you and the local representative from the animal shelter appeared to talk about animal abuse.

For all phases of the media, this kind of campaign works well.

Stumped on choosing a charity? Ask yourself these questions: Have you survived cancer or a heart attack? Are you diabetic? Did this play into your story? Have you been a victim of a violent crime? Did you use this experience in your story? Look to your own life to give the answers. They are there.

Preparing Your Press Kit

A press kit is a very, very valuable tool when it comes to self-promotion. It's what's going to introduce you to professionals who can help your career. From newspaper and magazine editors to television and radio producers, a press kit is your first introduction.

It's best to use a glossy, heavy-papered pocket folder. Buy the best you can, but don't get too fancy. You want something that showcases your professionalism.

Inside this folder you will need:

1. Your business card with accurate mailing address, phone numbers, including your cellular, and your e-mail.

2. An 8" X 10" glossy black-and-white photo of yourself.

3. A color copy of the cover of your book. If you are lucky enough to have a publisher who will provide extra covers for you, you have another blessing to count. If you want actual covers you will need to request them from your publisher months in advance of the book's release. I ask for one hundred and fifty, and I have usually gotten them.

4. If you have any previous print articles about yourself, this is the place to include them.

5. Your résumé. Keep it brief. Don't list your babysitting jobs, but do list your education and any new works you have in progress. Let the media see that there is a lot more to you than this one book.

6. A press release. This is the most important sheet in the package. This is your introduction, and, if at all possible, get as much professional input on this as you can. This is where that nonfiction spin on your romance book will come in. Work on this press release with your publicist until you are both very comfortable. It should include the "hook" that the media—whether radio, television, or print—will use to put you on their show. *No one is going to put you on his or her show because you wrote a romance novel.*

Media folks want something to talk about, so give it to them. If you want to include your work with a local charity or tie your donations of the royalties to your favorite charity, you need to mention it in the press kit. *NEVER promote a charity that you don't believe in your heart is worthy. Affiliating yourself with a charity or cause for the sake of publicity is a lie and it will undermine all your efforts. Be honest when dealing with the media. They are very savvy folks.*

If you truly don't have a nonfiction spin on your life or your book, remember that the fact that your book is being published is *news*. In many ways it has changed your life. You now have that experience to talk about. If you got a large advance, so much the better. The media *loves* the rags-to-riches story. If you don't know that J.K. Rowling was nearly destitute, caring for her small children and writing her books in the back of a coffee shop because it had heat and her apartment did not, you now should have a better appreciation of the Harry Potter creator. If you ever thought that God was unduly punishing you with adversity, it's not until you write your press release that you realize you can turn all those lemons into lemonade.

The press release should contain one sentence about your parents, your town of birth, and where you went to school, but that's all. Give no more than a one-paragraph or even a two-sentence pitch about your novel. Leave the storytelling until you are on the air.

This, then, will constitute the press kit you will send to radio and television stations. You do not have to spend a great deal of money on the portfolio itself. Even when I have hired a publicist and she pitched my work, the only cover on this press kit was a color Xerox of the cover of the book pasted onto the folder front.

I was on a book tour one year and happened to be in Portland, Oregon, at the exact same time as author James Patterson. For two days we showed up at the same radio stations, television stations, and hotels for the same interviewers to talk to us. I saw his press kit. WOW! It was the same kind of folder I had (the two-pocket jobbie), but his cover was glossy black with big embossed-gold letters for the title and looked exactly like the fabulous and very expensive book jacket his publisher had commissioned for his hardcover book.

You know how some women envy other women for their gold watches or diamond rings? I covet press kit covers.

When you read in *Publishers Weekly* that a certain publisher is spending a million dollars on an author's promotion, you can bet their press kit will knock the socks off any television junior producer.

Remember your competition when you are out there trying to promote yourself. Your press kit is going head to head with James Patterson and his big, bold, gold letters.

Keep the Scope Small to Score Big

In your grassroots campaign to self-promote, always start with your hometown first. Once you've gotten an article in a local newspaper or small business magazine or local advertising magazine, then expand again.

Use that article to move to the next biggest town in your state. Use the phone book to get the newspaper's number. Find out the name of the features editor. You can send your book to a book reviewer, but these tend to only be in large city publications like the *Chicago Tribune* or the *Los Angeles Times*. In smaller communities, you want to get a feature article written about you. We will expand upon these points further in this chapter.

Once you have the name of the features editor, find out his e-mail, if possible. This makes it easy for everyone. You can even attach photos of yourself along with your press kit.

You will need a dynamite lead-in for that editor to actually open up your e-mail. So, blowing a few things out of proportion isn't all bad. You're still telling the truth, but the press doesn't mind exaggeration at this stage of the game. Therefore: "Local Woman Hits It Big in the Big Apple" is corny, but it's just the kind of thing that will get you noticed. If your book is a foreign-set historical, try "Hailey Smith brings Ireland to Hometown, USA."

I did an entire grassroots tour one year when I moved from Houston back to my hometown in Indiana after my father passed away. I called it "Hometown Girl Returns to the Heartland." Is that corny or what? I nailed more than fifty radio shows and a dozen cable and television stations without the help of an expensive publicist. Granted, none of them were national shows like NPR, MSNBC, or CNN, which I've done since that time, but the people who will show up at the bookstore signing later that night listen to those local radio shows.

Tub-thumping and grassroots promotion for authors is never going to fade away. It is only going to get stronger in the years to come because, believe it or not, book signings are not only getting harder to book, but there is a great deal of talk within the larger chains that book signings are passé.

Authors just don't bring the crowds they used to, and the bookstores know it. Unless you are already established and fairly well known, you will find getting book signings quite difficult.

I had a very long discussion in person with a large, national chain-store manager who told me that very soon, his chain would only be looking at authors whom they could promote as "event authors." This kind of author would have to have written dozens of romance novels *or* "some novels, some nonfiction, a screenplay or two." I remember listening to this man rattle off a lifetime of work like it was as easy as planting a spring vegetable garden. *Okay, let's see. We'll have a half dozen mysteries, three screenplays, a dozen nonfiction, but only the inspirational variety of nonfiction books, and oh, a book of poetry would be nice.*

With the fall of the independent bookstore retailer in the mid-1990s, many new authors found themselves with no place to promote their books. Chains have to be booked four, five, six months in advance for a signing. I remember when you just called up and asked, and the manager booked the events. Now everything is run through corporate headquarters and it takes an act of Congress for my publicist just to get the signings booked. Even then, many chain stores will not book you unless you can prove that you have local or national media prior to the booking date.

The good news is that we are again seeing the rise of some independent bookstores.

I started with "used bookstores" for my signings many years ago. Frankly, these are the loveliest and most accommodating people on the planet. I bless every one of them everyday.

Yes, they are selling my old copies for a dime. Yes, their sales cut into my sales . . . sometimes. On the other hand, many of them are the very people that get a new reader "hooked" on your old books so much that when they do buy a new issue, they will look for your stories. These used bookstore owners are Mom and Pop, and they love to have events. Once you have your publishing date, call them up and see if you can get something booked. Many times they will have "event signings" in which they have a dozen or more authors sign at one time. They are the kind of hometown folks who serve punch and cookies to their clients. See what I mean? Angels, all of them.

Jump at the chance to participate. Be sure to bring the owner a box of chocolates or a nice dessert to add to her buffet. Ask if there is anything else you can provide, perhaps a balloon bouquet or some flowers. Make a friend of this person. They could be your biggest ally in the years to come in your career.

One more word about radio interviews: There is no such thing as a radio interview that isn't worthwhile. Many can be booked across the nation without you leaving your house. Live phoners are here to stay, thank goodness. My advice is do all you can to get on radio shows. It isn't easy to book them. That press kit you made will become incredibly important to you, because the station producers will judge your worth on what you put in the press kit. Remember, their job is to book interesting guests who will elicit a response from the listeners.

Tips and Techniques for Successful Self-Promotion

As simple as they seem, these marketing ideas will never go out of style, and they work:

* *Giveaways*. From pens and pencils with your name on them to bookmarks with your book cover (in color), to postcards you mail, to a mailing list starting with friends and relatives and bookstore owners and radio show hosts, the residuals probably will not come back to you on your first book, but if you remember you are planting the seeds for the rest of your career, this work is not in vain.

* *T-shirts*. If you do them, make sure they are good quality T-shirts. I had shirts that were embroidered with my book title made to give to on-air listeners and to bookstore managers or chain bookstore people. Yes, they were expensive for a T-shirt, but they were and are memorable.

* *Newsletters*. Do produce a newsletter if you have a fan base. You don't have to write one every month, but once or twice a year is nice if you have a new book coming out. If you don't have anything to publicize, don't waste your money paying for paper, toner, and stamps that won't result in sales.

* *Web site*. A must in today's world. No matter how much you spend or don't spend, put as much information about you and your book on the Web site as you can. Color photos are best. Make sure there is a color cover of your book. Have a way for your readers to e-mail you. Post your newsletter if you like. "My Web site is *www.mountainzenproductions.com*"

A word of warning: Two years ago, in the middle of my moving out of Texas, forming my film company, and a jillion other things, my Web site domain name came up for renewal and I missed it by one day. One day.

A pornography company bought my domain name and for a year if you went to *www.catherinelanigan.com*, you found pornography. It was a horrible experience for me and for my readers. Thankfully, I have a great IT guy now who keeps on top of that kind of thing for me and the second the domain name came up for renewal this year, I got my own name back. So, let that be a lesson to you if you do get a Web site up and running.

✤ *Thank-you notes.* Send them to everyone. Booksellers. Reviewers, if you can find an address for them. If you can't, see if you can send an e-mail or make a follow-up phone call. Thank everyone who helps you, especially your editor. This isn't just promotion. This is courtesy.

✤ *Print ads.* These are expensive and unless you have a very healthy bank account, you probably can't afford these. However, you can afford ads in Romance Writers of America's monthly report. You can afford ads in *Romantic Times Magazine* and they are effective.

✤ *Conventions.* For romance authors, the Romance Writers of America conventions are terrific. There are so many very good agents and editors who go to this national convention literally looking for that next shining literary star. Submit samples of your work for competitions. Send your work to the agents and then find out if they are going to the convention and set up an appointment with them to meet them face to face. If you're lucky, you'll get signed. If you are half lucky, you will find an agent or editor who has read your work and will honestly tell you what is wrong with your writing, how to improve the story, and what you can do to make that story saleable. That is the best scenario of all, believe me. We all learn from our mistakes, and these corrections you make with your writing now will enhance your writing and improve your chances of being published again and again.

Organizing Your Own Book Tour

Book tours can cost as little as two or three thousand dollars if you do the media booking yourself, drive your own car, and stay with friends while out of town.

If you do a larger book tour, the cost can be astronomical; the average is twenty-three thousand dollars for a ten-city tour, and will far outweigh any money you would make on the book, both in advances and in royalties. As time goes on and you write half a dozen books, you might begin to rethink how you want to handle the publicist question, but frankly, it should be dictated by dollars.

Just as you put your heart and soul into your book, you now have to put toil and sweat into promoting your book to the public. The more you do to self-promote, the more your publisher will sit up and take notice.

Your ability to promote can even be the deciding factor when the publishing board is voting on whether to buy your next book.

As always, if you do your best and do the work, it will pay off.

Plotting a Small, Effective Book Tour

Budget

Decide now how much money you can spend on a book tour. If you are working at a day job, the time you spend will have to be carved out of your weekend time, evenings, or vacation. Taking your vacation days is special to other family

Sidebar: Media Lists

You may or may not know that there is a major media list book called *Bacon's Directory*. This book costs several hundred dollars, and unless you intend to go into the publicity business, this is an expensive way to get information. However, if on your first book being published you already have strong interest from your publisher for a second or third book (this kind of editorial buying has been increasing in the past year or two), you might want to spend the money for this book.

You can buy bookstore and special-interest mailing lists. I have seen these lists cost as much as a thousand dollars.

PR newsletters such as *Lifestyle, Bulldog, Party Line, and Contact* have up-to-the minute information about media lists. They contain information about changes in staff in media across the country, the names of reporters who are looking for certain stories and more pertinent information. These publications cost money.

members, and this must be considered, as well. Make sure the family does not object. Here are some tips and things to keep in mind when it comes to planning out and sticking to a budget.

* How much will it cost in extra meals out when you are not there to cook? What babysitting services will you incur should you be on the road for two weeks?

* Gasoline, airfares, hotels, and meals cost money. To help you decide how to conduct your tour with greatest cost efficiency, a good rule to follow is, "if the distance can be covered in six hours or less . . . drive."

* Cut hotel costs by bunking out with friends and family in the area or around the state.

* Cut meal costs by taking your food with you on the road and skipping the restaurants, even the drive-thru kind. A cooler in the backseat with low-carb snacks and fresh fruits, carrots and celery, not only saves money but insures that by the time you are on television in Portland from your home in Sacramento, you will still fit into that new skirt you just bought.

* If you need to fly to a distant city for a great interview, fly coach, fly cheap, and book early. Unfortunately, this is hard to do in the media game because television seldom books more than two weeks out. Radio is different and will book months in advance. However, while you don't need to leave town for a radio gig, if you book a really great Barnes & Noble or high-profile independent bookstore for a signing, it would be wise for you to fly to that city and go to the station for the radio spot.

* Budget the cost of extra copies of your book that you will need to give to the radio announcer or to the television crew for them to put on the screen while you are on television.

* Press kits are important, as well as books. Print up several to take with you on tour even though you have sent them out to the station producers and CRRs you will be meeting. I recommend a dozen to two dozen. Have plenty of business cards.

Time Management

If booking a tour takes a publicist and her assistant two to three months of constant phone calling, you can expect to spend that much time on your tour, as well.

Time Rule #1: Keep Your Tour Small

This is your first book. You don't need a national tour to give your book a shot in the arm. This is also the time to simply test the waters of your own media and promotional abilities. Taking on too much can be as dangerous as not doing anything at all.

* Book the bookstores first.

* Ask your publishing house's publicity department if they would do this for you. Once the publisher knows that you are going to pay for a tour yourself, they will bend over backwards to help.

* If you get no cooperation (sometimes this does happen), then call the local chain's (Barnes & Noble, Borders, Bookstop, Bookstar, Hastings, Books-a-Million, Scribner's, Baker & Taylor, etc.) community relations reps. If they tell you that all signings have to be booked at the corporate level, then explain that this is your first book and you aren't getting the cooperation you would like from your corporate office. Then ask the rep if you could set up an appointment with them or take them to lunch. You are now working on your future business. One good, solid relationship with one CRR from even one local chain is invaluable to your career. Don't take "no" for an answer.

If the rep still is reluctant, ask if you can send her/him an autographed copy of your book.

NOTE: Most all bookstore employees, even the managers, have to buy their own books. When you can give them one free, they will always remember you. The point is that if they like it, they will recommend it to their staff, their readers, and their friends.

When you send the book, include a thank-you note, your business card, and any printed materials you have such as bookmarks (which I recommend because readers actually use them, as opposed to postcards they junk), pens, T-shirts, and book bags.

If you *still* don't get the booking, wait a few weeks for the rep to get your book and goodies, and then *call them back*. They may go to bat for you and call their corporate office themselves and set the date.

Time Rule #2: Booking Radio Is a Must

Chances are your first book is a rack paperback. Romance paperbacks have less than one month on the shelf to make their mark. That means you have to sell a lot of books very fast. Therefore, you don't need to worry about a radio show three months after your book has been published because the chances are the book won't be on the shelves when the listener/reader goes out to buy it.

NOTE: Your book WILL still be available on Amazon.com. If the radio is a live phoner, make sure you mention the fact that readers will have to order the book at the bookstore (this is very good for your future, by the way . . . that booksellers hear your name being ordered) and that listeners can order online at BN.com, Amazon.com, etc.

I have included here some tips that should help in booking your own radio spots.

❧ Listen to the radio talk shows in your area, and then use the phone book to get their numbers. Check out all the other radio and television stations in your town. Make a list.

❧ Start with the AM stations first, as they will have the talk shows where you are most likely to get a "gig."

❧ Call the station and ask the receptionist for the name of the talk show *producer*. Get that person's name and direct line if you can.

☙ Talk to the producer. Explain that you are a *local* author. You have just been published by a large New York publishing house. You have been involved with the local SPCA and you wondered if you could come on the show and talk about "loving the dogs and cats of our community." (Or mention the charity you have chosen or your cause. If it is cancer and your book comes out in October, that's National Breast Cancer month.) Explain that you have featured golden retrievers in your romance. Explain that you are donating a portion of your royalties to the local SPCA chapter.

☙ Book at least one AM talk show.

☙ Now call the producer of an FM station. They usually won't allow an author to come on, but explain to the producer that you want to come on the morning drive time show and *give away* four copies of your book to the listeners who call in. Radio stations are always looking for freebies to give to their listeners. If you can tie in your local charity or your cause célèbre to the pitch to the producer, so much the better. They will only give you a few minutes in between music and news, but that is all you need.

☙ Remember, you want the morning drive time slot . . . if possible. If the producer will only book you at midnight . . . TAKE IT!

☙ *You must never say "no" to a media gig.*

Time Rule #3: Print Media and Television Spots Are the Holy Grail

Don't be put off or frightened of television programs or the printed media. Again, start small and work with it. Over time you will become proficient with interviews that sell your books.

☙ Use the phone book to list all the newspapers and area "magazines." Get their fax numbers.

☙ You will now fax to all print media in your area. In this instance, fax statewide if you can. When starting at the grassroots level, it is best to book smaller cities and towns than to go for the larger cities. Every romance novelist who ever "made it big" had to start somewhere.

❦ Fax the big city newspapers and state magazines.

❦ You will need an attention-getting fax cover sheet and your fabulous bio page (or 1 1/2 pages, but no more).

(The following is an example of a press release I used in 1996 for my book *Dangerous Love* by MIRA Books.)

❦ You will title the fax cover page thus:

FOR IMMEDIATE RELEASE: CONTACT: Your Name
310-555-5555

GOODBYE SELF-SACRIFICE, HELLO SELF-EMPOWERMENT

DANGEROUS LOVE BY LOCAL AUTHOR CATHERINE LANIGAN
INTRODUCES INSPIRING NEW BREED OF HEROINE.

In Appendix A of this book, you will find the complete press release that should be faxed to newspapers and magazines. You will fax the complete release with the above caption on the fax cover sheet. Make certain you always have your contact information on both the fax cover sheet and the press release page.

❦ Using the fabulous single-page press kit bio that you have worked up, putting a nonfiction "spin" on you and your book, you will now fax that with this cover sheet to the features editor at all newspapers and magazines or periodicals.

❦ You will fax the talk show producers of the larger statewide radio stations, beginning with AM. You will request LIVE or TAPED PHONE-IN interviews. At the bottom of your fax, list any and all community work, charity affiliations, and make certain you stress the fact that you are a LOCAL AUTHOR. Even on the state level, you are still a local author.

Time Rule #4: Timing of Faxes Is Imperative

❦ Send all the faxes in one day. That way you can time the responses accurately. If you do not hear anything from anyone within *three* days, begin with your follow-up calls.

Time Rule #5: Always, Always Follow Up Your Faxes and Calls

♣ Be clear to state that you have a book signing at that city's independent/chain bookstore. You want to use their newspaper or talk show to promote that signing.

♣ The fact that you are from out of town and on a book tour and signing books in their city is a "news story." Use this line in your pitches.

Time Rule #6: Keep Your Schedule Tight and Focused

♣ You have booked your own town with two book signings, one radio interview, and one newspaper feature article.

♣ You have been able to book three surrounding towns with book signings and a couple more radio shows. All these towns can be reached in a day by car and you can be home at night.

♣ Watch your local television news shows and talk shows. Make a note of the host and the producer's names when the credits roll. Call your local station producer and "pitch" them. They may ask you for your press kit, and then send it. Follow the same process for surrounding cities.

♣ Let's say you have booked a national television affiliate (NBC) in Indianapolis, the largest major city within four hours. You call Aunt Sally and she'll put you up for two days. Now you need to get out a road map and chart another major city within four hours of Indianapolis. Now that you have one national affiliate station booked, use that "gig" to book Terre Haute, Indiana, or Cincinnati.

♣ Start the process over again. Get one book signing in that next city and then a radio show and shoot for a television interview.

This is exactly the process that a publicist would use to book your tour. The publicist has working relationships with the major television and radio talent in their home base city. Therefore, they have the opportunity to book the better shows. That does not mean that they will—just that they have the contacts to do so. Those contacts and their relationship is what you are paying for.

Now that you have your tour plotted out, try to keep your tour to no more than two weeks for a first book at this point.

While you are on tour, call your publicist at the publishing house and ask her if your sales are climbing. These days all publishing houses and sales departments are wired to the max. If they see "rate of movement" or "title velocity" this will make an impact on your book's ability to stay on the stands longer.

If the sales department sees that your book is being reordered a few weeks to a few months after it's release, the publisher will get behind your title in the way of more advertising, publicity, possibly even bankroll more of a book tour for you.

What to Do if the Idea of a Tour Is Out of the Question

Let's say you are terrified of a radio interview and there is absolutely no way you could handle a television interview. Or you have family obligations that prohibit your ability to leave the home, such as an invalid parent or sickly child.

In this case:

> ✤ Send faxes to local newspapers or magazines. You can still do interviews over the phone with a newspaper journalist.

> ✤ Send promotional materials to local independent bookstores.

> ✤ Send a copy of your book and promotional materials to the chain bookstore CRR.

> ✤ If you have the money for postage, etc., send your book and promotional materials to as many nearby city bookstores as possible. Be inventive with your cover letter. Include your bio and business card. If you have bookmarks printed up, AUTOGRAPH THEM and send a couple dozen to the CRR to dispense in the store.

Even though this is your first book, you will begin to build your own private media database. Building up a media list will serve you well as you write your second, third, and subsequent books. Here are some tips for making your list.

* Keep a separate file and accurate records of each CRR, producer, and radio show host you spoke with. Make certain you have their names correctly spelled.
* Start the file with the *type* of media outlet, such as network television, national radio (NPR, etc.), syndicated television or radio program, cable television, newspaper, or magazine.
* Make certain you have every phone number, e-mail, mailing address, and zip code for each.
* Every city's tourism agency or chamber of commerce has a local media list.
* Use maps to delineate your area of concentration. Use maps to give you a list of prospective cities you may not have considered visiting for a book signing.
* Remember that small towns will welcome you with open arms because "brand-name" authors do not usually go to smaller towns.
* Contact "resort" magazines in your area. They are always looking for "celebrities" who visit and their positive responses to the area and its amenities. (Perhaps you will want to "set" your next book in this resort area.)

Booking your own media is very time consuming and difficult, but take refuge in the fact that nearly every romance writer has done this hands-on legwork themselves in the beginning. This is not a horrible thing. This is your life. This is part of the fun of being a published romance author. Enjoy every breath of it. Years from now when you have written your twelfth novel and you have had all these years of practice, and doing television interviews is as easy as falling off a log, you will look back on these days with pride.

You pushed your own envelope and you succeeded!

Don't Wear that Antebellum Costume to the Book Fair

Many years ago when romance was struggling to find its way, and unfortunately, there were more bad agents than there were good ones, a lot of very good ladies and good writers were given bad advice about how to handle their careers.

Authors went to outrageous proportions to simply get attention for themselves and their books.

I've seen everything from wearing period costumes to workshops and dinner meetings to petulance, even temper tantrums with their editors, to outlandish and uncalled-for language in mixed company at gala charity functions.

All of this folderol to gain attention, when the answer is very simple: write better.

If you have to create a personality because you don't think you have one, don't start now that you have a professional audience.

Editors and agents love good writing. The bonus for them is if you happen to be pleasant, logical, and perhaps, if they are very lucky, fun to work with.

Self-promotion does not mean carrying a cockatoo on your shoulder to Book Expo America.

Self-promotion means knowing within the marrow of your bones that you were given talent to write and that you have the discipline to see the process through to the very end, perhaps for the rest of your life.

Carry yourself with dignity. Conduct your life with grace. It's the best dress to wear.

THIRTEEN

Building a Long-Term Career

*M*ake no mistake about it. The competition in the romance-writing field is intense. *Romantic Times* Magazine claims to review more than two hundred and fifty titles a month. That's more than three thousand titles a year. For every title that is published, there are scores of manuscripts that were read and rejected, and even more manuscripts are written and not submitted due to the very difficult task for aspiring authors to procure an agent.

The competition you will meet simply by trying to get your foot in the door is horrendous. It is not a venture for the meek of heart or spirit.

What many aspiring writers forget or simply don't realize is that writing is a business. They have read magazine articles or news reports that J.K. Rowling has earned more than one billion dollars from her *Harry Potter* series, and they are off to the typewriter.

If you start out expecting to make a million dollars per book you will be disappointed. Nine times out of ten if you expect to make more than your advance on your first book, you will be disappointed. Your publisher doesn't expect a miracle on your first shot out of the gate, why should you?

Your publisher is interested in building your career. What they are hoping is that your first book will get good reviews. Those reviews will help to generate good to strong presales to the distributors and the chain stores. If those presales are strong you will be given a good to large print run. This is the number of copies of the book that will be placed in the retail outlets. How does the publisher determine that vital print run number?

In the article by Deanna Carlyle, "Who's Got the Power? How a Publisher's Sales Force Can Make or Break Your Book," in the October 2003 *Romance Writer's Report*, Denise Little, a former buyer for a national bookstore chain, is quoted as saying, "The way the publishers set print run is to solicit their six or seven biggest accounts three to four months before the book goes on sale, and get estimated buys (which need to be accurate within 10 percent of the actual order, which comes in a month or so later) on the titles in their list. They add up these estimates, and that's what they use to set up the actual print run. Generally, these six or seven big accounts make up a reliable percentage of the total orders, so the publishers extrapolate from the estimates to get the total order."

You can see now that not only does the sales team or sales force play a key role in determining your print run numbers, but this print run can directly affect your book's chances of becoming a hit in the marketplace.

Traditional publishing thinking has always been that it takes a 250,000 first print run to even have a shot at the *New York Times* Best Seller List.

If your print run comes in at 40,000, don't panic.

Too many times a first-time author has been given an astronomical first print run and then the book didn't sell. This is called "poor sell-through." If this happens it could negatively impact your chances of ever being published again.

A good sell-through is 70 percent. Therefore, it is easier to reach that 70 percent goal with your 40,000 print run than it would be for that author (whom you were about to envy) who got a 250,000 print run.

Keep your eye on the print run you have. Use your promotion and book tour efforts to simply get your book off the shelves and achieve that 70 percent sell-through. It is a goal you can reach.

Many times, your publisher will not wait until your first book sells before she brings up the subject of your next book. If the publisher is pleased with your performance, that you turned your book in on time or close to your deadline, and that you have been pleasant and even fun to work with, then she will want to keep the momentum going if she's smart.

As I have mentioned in the early chapters of this book, your publisher is not interested in one book from you. She's looking for the person who can write twenty books over a couple of decades. The publisher is going to put a great deal of money into your first book. Your first book may be an ego boost to you, but it's a severe financial loss to the publisher in most cases. Their formula is to build your first book, get you some notoriety, and then make money on your second, third and fourth books. If you can write a book a year, the editor who "discovered" you has a feather in her cap.

Stay Focused on Your Own Career

To keep up with the intense competition of the publishing world, you must come to know your own literary voice as well as you know your own kids. As you become more comfortable with writing, learn to research better and faster, learn how to plot stories in your sleep, and come to know the exact words your inner voice is struggling to say, you are in the process of staying focused.

The problem with writing is that though it is a solitary life, the business and career demands of today's world are taking up more and more of an author's time and concentration.

Many times you will hear well-known authors complain that they spend half the time writing these days as they did in the beginning. That is because once you are established (and getting that first book sold is established), you must nurture the career part of your writing life.

But you also must be able to grow your talent and push the boundaries of your own mind to create something better each time you sit down to start a new novel. That will include better characterization, more intricate plots, and searing attention to details and research.

However, times change our styles just as much as the publishing house makes its voice known to us. Your career will be directly impacted by all kinds of changes in the future, and of those, you must at least be aware.

Where the New Competition Will Come From

I believe the days of the Barbara Cartland kind of romances, in which there was very little in the way of plot and the story climaxed only with the hero kissing the heroine at the point of the proposal, have passed with her. The public does not want the same story in a different setting told to them over and over by the same author, such as Barbara did for over forty years. Romances are exploding. More than any other genre of fiction or storytelling, romance is number one. I read an article once in the *Romance Writer's Report* in which Jayne Ann Krentz stated that she had a theory that romance was THE core story, always; that every genre emanated from the core love story.

Sidney Lumet, the great director, once said that there were only thirty-seven plotlines and they were all love stories. He said that every story for film or literature was a love story. Whether it was the love between woman and man, man and a dog, or a man and his country, they were still all love stories.

Remember when we asked you to look at the publisher's Web sites? Remember the Harlequin site? Just this year alone there are four new lines; HQN, Steeple Hill Love Inspired Suspense, Silhouette Bombshells, and Steeple Hill Café. If you were to look at an older Harlequin Web site, you might see the demise of a couple lines such as Super Historicals and Regencies.

Still need more ideas of what the competition will look like in the future?

Look to the example of cable television. Right now there are a couple hundred channels.

I was in a meeting only a month ago with industry professionals and discovered that within a year there will be over four thousand new satellite television channels available. Four thousand. Think about that. Couple that with three thousand romance titles a year and hundreds of feature films shown in theaters and straight to video or DVD. Your audience can find anything they want to suit their tastes at any given moment.

Your competition today is so diversified that if you truly did allow the competition to dictate your writing, you would have to write a dozen books a year, and that's just not humanly possible (unless you are Nora Roberts). There are, however, a number of things you can do to stay informed about the competition *and* stay focused on your own career:

Rule 1: Avoid the Competition Trap

Don't let the fact that there are thousands of romance books being published every year stop or impede your progress. It is easy to see why and how as a new author you could get caught in the competition trap. You're your own greatest competition. If you lose focus, even for a minute, your career could suffer.

The competition trap comes in when you spend more time watching all the other 1,340 romance authors' titles and their sales numbers or positions on the best-seller lists instead of doing what you are supposed to be doing: writing and self-promoting.

Obsessing over the success of other authors will make you crazy, and eventually, you can lose proper perspective.

Sadly, too many editors, agents, and other authors will cite the tale of a talented newcomer who self-sabotages their career by being vindictive, jealous, or bitter toward other authors who are selling better than they are. These comments come out during telephone conferences with the agent and with the editor.

I have been to conventions when a new author with great reviews came up to me and felt that it is her duty to fling her rave reviews in my face and then proceed to tell me how much better her story was than mine!

That is an example of getting caught in the competition trap.

If you are insecure about your new fame, such as it is, keep your "acting out" to yourself.

The rest of us authors have all been there. We were scared witless, too. We've been down the road you are about to travel, but it is a long, long way from having a number one best-seller on your first book out and still being around to publish your thirtieth book.

Some new authors get so crippled by the competition in romance that they are up against, they can't write anymore. This is a super shame. All that work and you are going to let the fact that someone has better sales figures than you, stop the creative energy and intuitive flow that God gave you? Shame on you.

The best advice is to leave the real competition watching to the professionals.

A Word on the Competition

If you spend your valuable time thinking and worrying about Suzy Q's book, you are not spending time on self-promotion. It is so easy to allow competition watching to become a personal obsession. You should always be aware of the current marketplace.

Try to incorporate the current market demands into the choice of setting and genre for your next book. You know that Regency and gothic romances are not going to sell to a publisher. Why would you buck the trend and spend a year of your life writing a book no one will buy?

Be smart. You must always write what is in your heart, but if you want to get into publishing and stay in publishing, then you must adapt to the marketplace. You can still write your story and be true to your heart.

Sidebar: The Publisher's Role in Competition Watching

Publishing houses never, ever let the competition out of their sight. The publisher is in the business of competition watching.

For instance, in the process of determining a print run for your book, the publisher must also decide if and how much money they will spend on your promotion.

They will look first to the strength of your book (reviews, editors' comments, etc.) and its sales potential.

They will look to the competition with similar titles and what kinds of sales those books had. They will look within their own company at titles similar to yours and check those numbers.

They will determine the salability of the subject matter contained in your book and finally, the strength of the final manuscript.

Now you can see how important the quality of your writing is, along with the genre you choose and the setting for the story. All these factors are going to be considered when the sales force is sitting around their conference table to determine how many copies they will print of your book.

Let's say that the marketplace is primed for your contemporary (remember there are two contemporaries for every historical) romantic thriller. The sales department may determine that this is a great time to launch and build your career. They may ask the marketing department to spend more money on your book rather than Suzy Q, who already has a big name and doesn't need the "push."

In the same *Romance Writer's Report* article mentioned on page 172, Denise Little explains that big chain buyers absolutely impact a book's promotional budget, even for first-time writers.

"There were many, many times when what I did as a buyer had a direct impact on what a publisher did with a book. It was particularly effective with first-time writers. If I loved a galley, I could take the book in quantity and arrange in-store promotions. Diana Gabaldon and Antoinette Stockenberg were among the authors that I pushed from book one."

The large publisher's sales departments are wired to the Internet and that gives them an advantage over all their competition, especially the small presses, because they can track a book's sales numbers on a daily basis.

If you, as the author, did this, you would develop an ulcer. Furthermore, you don't have this kind of access to a publisher's in-house numbers.

Calling the Editor

Don't call your editor to see how your book is selling. Chances are your publisher prints a minimum of a dozen titles a month. She/he has no idea if your book is selling its first week out, UNLESS, there was a huge print run (not likely on a first book) and your editor especially, is praying for a *New York Times* Best Seller slot for you.

Booksellers as Gauges

This is a better bet. While you are signing your book at your lovely book signing, ask the store manager what the sales have looked like. Did they put the book out early? Did any copies sell before your arrival? Has anyone called the store and said they "heard you on the radio"? What does the bookseller think of the cover?

When you present the store manager or the CRR with their own copy of the book, call them a month later and ask if they had a chance to read it. If they liked it would they recommend it to their shoppers?

Appreciation

Once your book has been out for a month or so, send a thank-you note to all the CRRs you met in person. This is the time to ask them, very diplomatically, for any more help. If the book sold out and you know this from your conversation with them a week or so after you were in the store, ask if they will reorder the book. Even if it's four copies it is a reorder.

Rule 2: Know and Learn from Your Competition

Rather than watching sales figures, it would better serve you to read other romance authors. A good idea is to read the authors of a certain *publishing house* in clusters, if possible, to get a bead on what that publisher is doing. If the competition's publisher just spent a hundred thousand on a particular author's advance, and then another two hundred and fifty thousand on publicity and advertising, or if the publisher is hyping a new sub-genre, then you should take notice. Why would you want to know this?

There is always the chance that you may want to switch publishers later in your career. Or if you find that you can write more than one book a year and your current publisher, who just produced your first book, says they don't want to publish more than one book from you a year, you should talk to your agent about submitting your other work to another publisher.

This is also the time to bring up writing under a pseudonym. Twenty years ago nearly every romance author published in New York wrote under a pseudonym. Jayne Ann Krentz is Amanda Quick and still uses Jayne Castle.

When you read other authors to get a flavor of their work or to explore what the publisher likes in their authors' work, pay attention to the depth of character and the depth of research you see in the book. Is it better than yours? How can you improve your own writing by their example? Do you need to research your subject matter more thoroughly?

Is the story long on action, dialogue, and over-the-top characters? Is the story cute and fun, but not particularly deep or insightful?

Does this publisher tend to publish more intellectually written romances? Do these books compare to the current literary novels of Joan Didion or Joyce Carol Oates?

Does the publisher appear to favor authors who write series books like Catherine Coulter or Janet Evanovich?

When you read authors grouped by publisher, you will begin to see writing in yet another vein. You will no longer view authors and their specific titles as stand-alone entities, but as part of a publishing house. Just as large houses like Harlequin have specific guidelines for certain imprints, you will see that publishing houses have a particular identity that they like to portray.

Rule 3: Watch for Branding

Branding in publishing, just like in the American marketplace, is the categorizing of a certain name with a certain product. Branding is usually the word used by a publisher for excellence and high quality. A Danielle Steele novel is usually a story of a certain kind of tough heroine who has to overcome some pretty tough odds. She is a "household name" for romantic contemporary stories, she has sold hundreds of millions of books worldwide, and she is known in just about every country on the globe.

Her books are very different from Debbie Macomber, who writes very sweet, sentimental stories. Debbie Macomber is known all over this hemisphere, and has sold hundreds of millions of novels, but she is not as well known as Danielle Steele. In fact, no one is as well known as Danielle Steele in romance.

Brand-name authors tend to write the same kind of story every time they sit down to write. Seldom do they make a real change in their stories.

When a reader picks up a Danielle Steele book, she knows exactly what she's getting.

Your publisher makes a great deal of money once you become branded, because they don't have to reinvent your wheel. You write one kind of story, and they are just fine with that.

However, there are problems inherent in branding.

For one thing, if the public tires of your continued same style, they won't buy another book.

You could get tired of altered writing the same story over and over, with just a few character changes and altering the locations. When this happens . . . the book will bomb.

I don't care how solid and old a brand-name author's name is; every once in a while they will write a dud. It happens. If the publisher believes that the story is not that strong and that there is the possibility that the reviews will be bad, in today's splintered and very discerning and informed consumer market-place, that publisher is not going to spend a great deal of promotional dollars on that book.

If the author is strong enough, one bomb won't hurt. But if it becomes two or three . . . this is a signal to both you the writer and to the publisher that you both need to make changes. Sometimes making the change is very painful and costly to you because you lost your contract, and to the publisher because they invested a great deal of time and money in you.

However, you are not out of the game. You just have to realize you are the pitcher, not first baseman.

All writing careers go up and down to a degree. All writers, especially romance writers, have to make changes. This is growth. This is extension.

It's a bumpy ride, but it can be a lot of fun.

Rule 4: Be Aware of Your Category's Trends

Trends within the publishing industry are constantly evolving, and it's impor-tant to understand what they are—this is your professional field, after all. However, if you start writing to satisfy a trend, the odds are the trend will be long over by the time you finish writing.

When the Cold War ended with the breakup of Russia a decade ago, romance suspense and thriller novels involving espionage and Russian/American spies hit the skids.

This kind of "publishing trend" has occurred many times in the romance genre, as I have mentioned. In the '60s and early '70s, gothic romances were all the rage. By the end of the '70s you couldn't find them anywhere. In the late '70s to mid-'80s the romance "bodice rippers" featuring pirates and abduction were so hot, publishers couldn't find enough authors to pump them out fast enough. Within less than a decade, the trend vanished.

In order to make money, which is always the bottom line in publishing, the publisher must do all they can to reach as broad a mass market as possible.

The publisher is taking a huge financial gamble on you that your story will sell. In the beginning of your career, the name of the game is survival. After you are established, the game turns to "flourish." Your publisher believes that in a few years, with three or four books under your belt, your numbers are going to rise. They have surefire business strategies to accomplish just that.

Career-Building Strategies

To help you manage your time and your career better, keep the following tips in mind. These can be done on a daily, weekly, or monthly basis, and they should be done in addition to your daily writing—not *instead* of it:

❧ Shop for an agent. This is a long process, so start now.

❧ Ask for advice from other authors about their agents.

❧ List questions you want to ask potential agents.

❧ Devise a query letter about your novel to show to prospective agents.

If you are just starting out, and I assume most of you who are reading this book are, then the agent issue is extremely important (as you know from chapter 10). The bottom line is that on a weekly basis, it does you no good to pour your heart out onto blank pages in your computer if you don't intend for people to read it. Finding an agent and the development of a strong, lasting relationship is a top priority.

You should also practice writing your own bio. List your history and, in a storytelling fashion, relate an anecdote about yourself that might be of interest to the public.

Then after you write the bio, write a future press release for yourself and your book. In the appendix you will find a sample of a professionally written press release.

Once a month you should work on a public relations or publicity campaign you would employ to sell your book. Check out local radio shows. Listen to the social/political slant of the talk show host. Is there any angle that you can use to get on this person's show? Are there any talk show hosts that you particularly like? If there are, follow this radio personality. Is he or she going to appear at a local fund-raiser? Can you buy a ticket to the fund-raiser and try to meet this person? In most communities, both local radio and television personalities are called upon or paid to MC or appear at area fund-raisers. These could be anything from a gala ball for the American Heart Association to the local fire-fighters' pancake breakfast.

Listen to the radio stations you might not ordinarily listen to. Plot out which ones you'd like to be on to promote your book.

Ask your local independent bookstores if they would let you do a signing once your book is published. Take the names of the store representatives for future contact. Leave them your business card.

Monthly, take the time to go online to find as many statewide newspapers you can find. Inquire if any would run announcements about you, the book, or a book signing, if you had one.

It is my bet that right about now you are asking yourself, what in the world is Catherine talking about? I haven't even finished the first chapter of my book.

I'm telling you these hints or tricks because I want you to start visualizing yourself as a published author. "If you can conceive it, you will live it."

You must prepare your own way. No one is going to do it for you. Do the work and *it will happen*.

Every single month, without fail, do something very special for your family and/or friends who are supporting your efforts. Their love is more important than this book. Even if you don't finish your book this year, you will finish it in a year and a half. I promise. You only have one chance with your family. The kids will grow up and leave. Your husband or wife will get older. Your parents will die. Love them. That's the real romance.

Once a month promise yourself a veg day. Go to a movie, give a party, drive out to the country. Free your head. Your story will love you for it.

Do not neglect your bills, the trash, the laundry, your pets, your neighbors, or your community. You will glean your next plot and characters from all of them.

Never Stop Networking

Because there are thousands of romance authors and aspiring authors, this group has "managed" itself like no other group. Ask any business executive in the world of commerce who networks best, men or women, and the answer is always going to be women.

Women have been communicators since God created Eve. We know that to get something done we have to be curious about others, their interests, and in the process of asking another person about themselves, we find common goals, common concerns. This is networking.

Most women aren't afraid to ask questions. This definitely helps when you are networking. It always pays to keep your eyes and ears open; then once you do that, don't be afraid to open your mouth to promote your work. Then once you do that, offer to help the other person or persons.

The largest organized writer's group in the world is Romance Writers of America. Despite the title, RWA has chapters all over the world and the membership is over 8,500. The Romance Writers of America was founded in 1980 in Houston, Texas, by Rita Clay Estrada, Rita Gallagher, Parris Afton Bonds, Sondra Stafford, and Peggy Cleaves. The headquarters are at 16000 Stuebner Airline Road, Suite 140, Spring, Texas 77379.

If you are reading this book, I cannot stress strongly enough the benefits you will derive from being a member of Romance Writers of America.

If you live in a larger city you will undoubtedly find a local chapter, which you can join and get immediate help with your writing. These groups are phenomenal in that you will meet other writers who are struggling with their writing, as well. You can get your book critiqued within your group.

Best of all, once a member, you can submit your work for one of the many writing contests that RWA sponsors. The Golden Heart Award is open to writers who have not accepted a publishing offer for any novel or novella by a RITA-eligible publisher (A RITA-eligible publisher is defined as a nonsubsidy, nonvanity publisher that has released books on a regular basis via national distribution for a minimum of one year and has sold a minimum of 1,500 hardcover/trade paperback copies or 5,000 copies of any other format of a single fiction book or novella or collection of novellas in book form.)

The purpose of the RITA and Golden Heart "is to promote excellence in the romance genre by recognizing outstanding romance books and manuscripts."

The entrants for the Golden Heart must retain all rights to the entry and not have granted any of them to a publisher or any other party by the contest entry deadline.

The entire list of requirements and rules for entering your work, which, by the way, *is open to nonmembers*, is at the RWA's Web site—*www.rwanational.org*.

The point for you to understand here is that even if you entered your manuscript in the contest this year and lost, and you went back and rewrote the book, you can enter the same book again next year, as long as you did not get it published.

Publishers, agents, and editors pay attention to these national awards. There are other awards once you are published, such as the Janet Daily Award for Excellence, *ForeWord* Magazine's Book of the Year Romance Award, Reader's Preference Book of the Year Romance Award, and others.

All these contests have their own criteria. They all are valuable tools for the marketing of your book, for self-promotion, and to generate interest in your next manuscript from your current publisher.

In addition, as we mentioned, various states and chapters of RWA hold their own romance writing contest. Virginia, for example, bestows the HOLT Medallion in twelve categories of romance and romance sub-genres. In Virginia, there is one winner per category and four finalists.

The North Louisiana StoryTellers and Authors of Romance give The Suzannah Award.

The Couer de Louisiane RWA sponsors the Romancing the Tome contest.

In the state of New York is the Hudson Valley chapter of RWA, and they grant the Hook, Line, and Sinker.

Who is judging these contests? In nearly every instance of regional contests, the various categories are judged by "trained, published" authors in their respective categories. In many of the contests, the final decision is made by a large publishing house's editor, such as Ann Leslie Tuttle at Harlequin, who judged the Valentines Over Vegas Feel the Magic contest for the Cactus Rose chapter of RWA. The Romancing the Tome contest had Brenda Chin of Harlequin, May Chen of AVON Books, Anna Genoese of TOR Books.

These chapters pride themselves on procuring the respect of agents and editors to be their final judges.

This is one of the best ways to get your work to an agent or editor. In several chapters we have addressed this very point. The bottom line is, agents are looking for good writers. Agents need product to sell and they need good if not great books to keep their lights turned on and their staff paid. Agents have certain conventions they never miss. Agents are called upon not only to judge new writers' manuscripts but also to conduct workshops at romance writers' conventions. It is their job to be on the lookout for new talent. In speaking with many agents over the years, they have expressed real interest in the writers they meet at conventions.

You can query agents forever and not get the results you seek. If that is the case, then it is strongly recommended you do everything you can to join a RWA chapter near you and then go to the meetings and workshops. Learn what you can from those who are critiquing your work. Do the rewrite necessary, and then when that next chapter convention rolls around, enter your manuscript in the Golden Heart Award contest. If your work gets past the initial judging, which in most cases is conducted by published authors from your state, then by virtue of being a finalist, your work will be assessed by a bona fide agent and/or an editor from a major publishing house.

Romance Writers Report

There are many writers who cannot make the RWA chapter meetings, or there is not a group near their hometown. In this case, as a member of Romance Writers of America, every month you are sent the *RWR* newsletter, which is a magazine, really. It is an in-depth review each month of industry updates and news. You will find articles on writing that are very well written by published authors and editors from the top publishing houses.

One of the greatest values of the *RWR* is the articles concerning legal issues, written by qualified and respected literary attorneys on the subjects that will concern you and your career in the future such as: contracts, intellectual rights, foreign rights, film rights, and just about any issue that you have thought about. You will also find pro and con debates on legal issues you never thought about, and those are the ones of most interest.

The yearly dues are seventy-five to one hundred dollars. You will receive thousands of dollars' worth of information, meet new friends at the chapter meetings, and gain insights and strategies for your future in romance writing.

There is no other organization in the world that takes its memberships' dreams to heart like the Romance Writers of America. Frankly, there just are not any drawbacks to being a Romance Writers of America member.

FOURTEEN

In Spiritu

In spiritu means "the divine breath." As an author, artist, musician, or sculptor, all persons involved with the creative arts, at one time or another, experience a particular project that feels as if they are being led by the divine to create.

Inspiration is not something we earn or "are due." It is what it is . . . a gift from God. For most of us, this powerful flow of ideas comes intermittently. We cannot predict its entry into our lives, nor do we know how long it will last. Some people are quite super-stitious about inspiration. We've all seen sports stars who carry "lucky" rabbit's feet, wear a particular religious symbol around their neck, or use a "lucky" bat. I've heard of writers who have a particular type-writer they feel carries a certain power for them, but that kind of person is few and far between. I've read and interviewed many romance authors and pretty much we are all addicted to words. We write on anything that is handy when inspiration strikes.

I believe luck plays only a small part in our lives. I believe that everything is all meant to be, from the car not starting in the morning that makes you late for your appointment to the four-book deal you just signed with a publisher.

The only person who can stop you is you.

There is no rhyme or reason to the enormous flow of energy through us. However, we all know that particular feeling when it's within us. It is the reason we are obsessed with finishing a certain book no matter how tired or hungry we are. We will write endlessly. We claim we are in a "zone," and perhaps that is precisely what it is: a parallel dimension or state of existence.

Sometimes you will hear authors say, "The pages seemed to have written themselves."

Not all novels are like this, and after you've written a couple you may find that the first one came easily to you. The characters were more alive than your next-door neighbors or the lady who lives down the hall. Your second book could be a tug-of-war trying to get each paragraph to the page.

No one ever knows why this is, but the fact of the matter is, all of this is part of the artist's life.

The closer you can come to connecting with the divine in your life, the more in sync you will be with your own creative flow. I will refrain from mention of any particular religion, because what I am talking about is not religion. It is about what I perceive as God as far as my creativity is concerned, but an atheist would disagree with me. They might say that this creative energy is just that— some kind of energy field that the particular author can "tap" into and use to help them create a book or painting. I believe it is just that and more. I believe this power to co-create is part of our divine mission from God even before the day we were born. I think that our lives are divinely led and protected. We have the freedom of choice not to follow that path and that is when we buy into fear.

For the creative artist, fear is evil. It is the thief that steals your passion, your drive, and ambition. It is the witch that turns your passion into self-absorbed obsession when it was meant to be your unselfish gift to the world. When you release your book to your agent and publisher, you are "letting go" in a most profound sense. In a very real sense, you have "surrendered" to the power of the divine to do with your story what will be done. Writing is the most intimate work a person can perform, even more so than music or painting. Words are precise. Language is an exact code with which communication to all peoples is possible. To report and inform is the work of a journalist. To alter perspective and even to inspire is the work of the literary artist. To create good and evil, conflict and resolve, pain, heartache, and love, you, the author, in order to bring emotion to your story, must have endured a good many emotions and experiences in order to write about them.

The novel that portrays a heroine's loss of a child, when written by a woman or man who has endured this torture and its devastating grief, should relate firsthand what that experience was like. It is through the author's suffering that the audience "lives" a novel. If the author has "surrendered" to her own talent, and has not gotten in the way of divine flow, then the audience will receive inspiration for their own lives through the author's efforts and the words she has put on paper.

Though we call our romance novels "fiction," when you get down to it, little within the pages is truly fantasy. When writers expose themselves in confidence to an interviewer, most will admit that there is always a part of themselves in their characters. This goes for the heroes and the villains.

To create a real-sounding character with depth and those qualities that make that protagonist memorable, the author must learn to "bleed" onto the pages. If the author has endured hardships in his or her own life, these trials and tragedies are the echoes that will ring in the visceral chord of the public.

I have mentioned various authors of classics throughout time who have endured poverty, loss of family through death, or personal physical illness. They had the courage to sit down and continue writing through their pain until they finished putting it all on paper.

The lifetime trial of a human being is one of pain, sorrow, grief, happiness, joy, and abundance. All of us will experience each of these emotions and more, sometimes within the span of a single day. However, very few were given a talent for writing. Even fewer still were given a talent so great that their story will endure for generations.

I believe that all of you reading this book have been given the challenge to write a novel that will endure for all time. You wouldn't be searching through the book stacks to find guidance as is found in this book if you didn't have passion—if you didn't have the intelligence to know that it takes a great deal of knowledge and skill just to write well, much less find information about the publishing world to get published and stay published.

I believe that within your soul is eternal, radiant divine energy that will see your project through to its fruitful and flourishing end. This energy will give you courage to develop the very thick skin you will need to stand up to the rejections you will receive. It will give you courage and impetus to join a writer's group, take creative writing classes, and take acting classes for television interviews you will have to promote your book, and it will inspire you to write the next book.

Most importantly, I believe that writing romance is a greater calling than writing any other kind of fiction. In this new world of the new millennium, our technology has not only brought our world closer together, but it has exposed us and our children to minute by minute accounts of torture, warfare, political unrest, and violence never before seen by so many. Human beings burned alive are videotaped on the spot, and the footage is sent around the world instantaneously.

With computer-generated graphics, our movies are able to re-create ancient warfare in which hand-to-hand combat, beheadings, and mutilations by the thousands are possible. The films are so real, the screens so big, and the sound so perfect that as we view these films, we are "in it" with them, as F. Scott Fitzgerald so aptly wrote in *Tender Is the Night*.

There are few places in our entertainment where we can go to find the greatest virtue of all: *love*.

Even though you are starting out to write what you believed (before reading this book, I hope) was just a simple love story, I hope that I have given you a glimpse of how far your writing will take you.

When I wrote my first book I had met another writer who encouraged me not only to put my story on paper, but also to mail it to him to be critiqued. A month later, he phoned me to tell me that he had read my book and thought it was good. He had sent it to his agent in New York and she was going to call me in half an hour. Kathy Robbins of the Robbins Agency called me and told me she wanted to put me under contract. I called to thank the writer who had sent my book to her. I will never forget his words: "Writing will open up worlds to you that you never dreamed possible."

Back then, I could only guess at what those worlds would be. I fantasized about travel to foreign countries, as most all of us hope we get that chance to do. What I didn't realize was that my writing would open worlds inside my head and allow me to explore my own psyche, my talent, and to believe in the prayer of a more peaceful and love-filled world vision I hold for my granddaughter and her generation.

I take the responsibility of writing to heart, which I hope all of you do as well. Romance writing is as old as the first Greek myths and plays. It is the one genre that has continued to endure through the Middle Ages, through the Enlightenment period, and flourishes today.

Love is what romance is all about. Love is what human beings are capable of experiencing every day, but we don't. Love is the energy that is as close as we can aspire to God or the divine, yet we fill our lives with gossip, backstabbing, and selfish actions, which are the wedges that shatter our lives.

It's little wonder the sale of romance books is as solid as it is and rising all the time.

To write about love is to do your part to change the world for the better.

To aspire to write about the kind of romantic love that brings a man and a woman together to create a haven of pure energy within which their lives can *thrive* is a gift.

In your writing career, journalists, neighbors, critics, and even some family members will belittle you for writing romance. You will be told you don't write "real books." The condescension you will face sometimes will make your face turn red and you may even want to give up.

Don't.

The world doesn't need another romance book, it needs thousands more . . . worldwide.

Your calling is not small. One more romance book may not save nations from war, but it may save one woman's marriage or even her life. That woman may have children and you may save that woman's children. You may even save a man's life because you saved that woman's life.

Sound too far-fetched? You should read the wrenching letters I've received over the years, especially when the issues within the romance are domestic abuse and child abuse. My author friends who have sold millions of books will attest to the same observation about their readers.

When your life draws to a close, one of the questions you will ask of yourself is, "Did I make a difference?"

If you write romance, no matter what your sales figures are—big or small—you will know that you did make a difference.

You wrote about love.

Love will always change the world for the better.

APPENDIX A

Sample Professional Press Release

BLANCO AND PEACE ENTERPRISES LTD.
PUBLICITY PUBLIC RELATIONS PROMOTIONS
359 W. CHICAGO AVENUE, SUITE 200, CHICAGO, IL 60610

FOR IMMEDIATE RELEASE: CONTACT: Lissy Peace
                                                          312-573-2070

GOODBYE SELF-SACRIFICE, HELLO SELF-EMPOWERMENT

Dangerous Love BY CATHERINE LANIGAN
INTRODUCES INSPIRING NEW BREED OF HEROINE

The self-sacrificing heroine of much contemporary fiction may soon be a thing of the past; that is, if best-selling author Catherine Lanigan has anything to say about it. In her forthcoming book *Dangerous Love* (MIRA Books, August 1996; $5.99), Lanigan introduces an inspiring new breed of heroine into the literary fold: the "evolving woman."

Finding herself imprisoned by circumstances that are destroying who she is inside, the "evolving woman" builds an internal arsenal of wisdom, courage, and dignity that frees her to finally be true to herself. From self-sacrificing to self-empowering, she learns how to make choices that enable her to nourish her own soul, and as a result, fortify her capacity for nurturing those she loves.

In *Dangerous Love*, Lanigan presents three such compelling heroines whose lives form the edges of a tapestry of love and betrayal, woven by the one man who nearly destroyed them all. Yet for these remarkable women, the cause of their pain becomes the catalyst of their rebirth.

Sexy, seductive, and insidious, Richard Bartlow donned vulnerability like an expensive suit worn to impress the unsuspecting. He was addictive. The more a woman sacrificed for him, the less he cared, and the harder she tried.

Mary Grace, the bitter emotionally starved wife who gave up her future for promises never kept; Alicia, the desperate other woman and struggling careerist who saved Richard from ruin, at a tragic price; and Michelle, the luminous young beauty, for whom rape would have been a gentler fate. When they meet for the first time at Richard's funeral, they discover what they've been isn't necessarily who they are and that death is not always as final as it seems.

In addition to addressing self-empowerment in *Dangerous Love*, Catherine Lanigan, a longtime spokesperson for literacy programs and women's shelters across the United States, spotlights women's education as one of the key issues propelling her story lines.

"I wanted to create heroines whose characters were defined by their profound struggle to nourish and protect their sense of self, despite the impact of betrayal, abuse, and self-sabotage," comments Catherine Lanigan. "If this book helps just one woman come to grips with her own situation, or gently pushes her in the direction of self-empowerment, it will have all been worth it," she concludes.

Catherine Lanigan is the author of twenty-five other books, including the novelizations of *Romancing the Stone* and *The Jewel of the Nile*, which proceeded the blockbuster films of the same names.

APPENDIX B

California Moon Story Synopsis

Shreveport, Louisiana, Early November.

At the Sabine River Bridge, two American men are being brutally beaten by three South American men. Continually, the victims are asked, "Where is it?"

Neither American man answers satisfactorily. Finally, the two American men are placed in the front seat of a rental car. Both are comatose. One of the thugs starts the car, puts it into drive, and the car goes crashing over the bridge into the river. The three South American hit men get in their Mercedes and speed away.

Shannon Riley, thirty-five, a nurse at St. Christopher's Charity Hospital, is pulling her third in a row shift when the two men are brought into her emergency room. One man is dead on arrival. The other John Doe is fighting for his life.

For over a month, John Doe remains in a coma, and Shannon is assigned to his case. This man who apparently has no identification and has had no family or friends reporting him as missing fascinates her.

A loner herself, Shannon does her job, but for four years at the hospital, she has steered clear of any kind of relationship with a man or even with coworkers. She is as much a mystery to the staff at the hospital as John Doe is to the police. Shannon Riley and John Doe have a lot in common in that regard, even if John is still unconscious and doesn't know it.

To pass the time, Shannon creates a fantasy about John and invents a background for him. Even she does not realize she is starting to fall in love with her own fantasy.

Ben Richards, thirty-five, handsome, street smart, and an undercover FBI agent posing as a deputy for the local sheriff, is also assigned to John Doe's case. Ben has discovered that the other John Doe is Adam Rivers, a wealthy New Orleans attorney, who had lied to his pregnant wife about his trip to Shreveport. There are many mysteries and dangerous secrets whirling around the comatose John Doe, and Ben Richards is quite anxious to find the answers. While he is watching John, Ben finds himself attracted to pretty Shannon Riley; however, she is adamant that she is not interested in Ben as a potential boyfriend or even a friend. She is civil to him, but that is all. She shares no small talk with Ben, not even about the weather. More than being challenged by Shannon's silence, Ben is suspicious. His instincts about such things have never been wrong, and right now his radar has gone to alert status.

One day, John comes around, and using a hypodermic with an air bubble angled at Shannon's jugular, he convinces her that he will inject the air bubble into her bloodstream if she does not help him get past the guard at the door. Terrified and fearing for her life, Shannon agrees to help John. Shannon calls to Ben Richards, who is just outside the door. Ben comes in; John hits him over the head and takes Ben's gun.

One of the young nurses, Chelsea, gets in John's way as he makes his escape with Shannon still at gunpoint and nearly gets killed. However, Shannon thinks fast and saves Chelsea from death.

Lesson number one that Shannon learns: don't trust John Doe.

A high-speed chase ensues as Shannon and John speed out of town in Shannon's car. Twice they steal cars from unsuspecting citizens as they make their way to Dallas.

In Shreveport, the local sheriff, Jimmy Joe Bremen, is not asking the right questions of the right people, Ben Richards thinks. Rather than call his superior on the matter, Ben launches into an investigation of his own. While the rest of the sheriff's office is investigating John Doe, Ben goes to Shannon's apartment, breaks in, and takes a lot of notes. He discovers a woman with virtually no past. Her furniture is minimal; she has only a cat to keep her company. There are no books, no albums, no family photos, and no numbers on her speed dial.

Ben believes Shannon is hiding as much as or more than John Doe. His own dark humor is titillated as Ben uses every minute of his off hours and some of his duty time to investigate Shannon Riley.

Once Shannon and John Doe get to Dallas, John is having a difficult time recovering from his month-long recuperation. His muscles have atrophied and his energy level is nil. Threatening Shannon with the gun, he forces her to inject him with the medication he needs to keep going. The "caregiver" side of her takes over in that she administers antibiotics and vitamins to John. At the same time she is torn by her own instinct to survive. She tries several times to "trick" John and escape, but each time, he catches her in the act.

While driving, John explains that he is only an insurance salesman and that somehow he's gotten caught in what he thinks is a drug ring that his friend, Adam Rivers, was very much a part of.

In the process of putting the pieces of his memory back together, John reveals that his real identity is Gabe Turner. The men who beat him wanted a computer disk that Adam had given him. However, only hours before, Gabe had put the disk in a windbreaker and dropped it off at the cleaners. Then Gabe forces Shannon to take him to the Regency Cleaners in Dallas to retrieve his jacket and the disk.

New Orleans, Louisiana

Congressman Blane Blair sits in his lush office across from a well-dressed handsome Colombian wearing a fedora. Sardia is the coldest killer Alejandro Cassalia owns. Blane Blair knows that Sardia is there to kill him. Blane quickly explains that he was aware that Adam Rivers was washing money for Alejandro. However, he did not know that Adam was stealing from Alejandro. Blane did not think Adam was that stupid. Obviously, he was.

Blane promises Sardia that he will help contain this "trouble" in the United States and that he will do all he can to find the disk that contains the names of all the accounts into which Adam had placed Alejandro's drug money.

Sardia leaves, convinced that his boss's interests are best served today by not killing a congressman.

Texas Highways, December

While speeding through the South countryside, Gabe discovers that Shannon is a woman whose past contains as much murder and intrigue as what they are running from. For Shannon, her past and its sins lie in California, exactly where they are headed.

One particular night, Shannon explains that she was once married to a young, wealthy California politician. David Randall's mother, Amelia, had planned from the day of his birth that he would be governor. When David fell for Kathleen (Shannon Riley) and ran off in his last year at Stanford and married her, Amelia nearly lost her mind. To make matters worse, Kathleen became pregnant on her wedding night. Rather than the Randall family being pleased about their grandchild, Amelia tried to pay Kathleen off to leave David and let Amelia adopt the baby. Once Laird is born, David's drug habits come to light. He buys his cocaine from Alejandro Cassalia's henchman, Sardia. But when David's habit becomes too expensive and he can't pay up, Sardia rigs the car that David, Kathleen, and little Laird are driving in.

On a mountain pass, the car's brakes fail, and it skids, slams into the mountainside, and bursts into flames. Kathleen succeeds in saving Laird from the flames, but not David. The baby is badly burned and will be disfigured for life. Though Shannon is burned and hospitalized, Amelia convinces Shannon to give up the baby to her so that she and her great wealth can save Laird's life. Shannon believes that somehow Amelia could buy an arrest of drunken driving charges to be brought against Kathleen. Kathleen changes her name to Shannon Riley and disappears in the Louisiana city of Shreveport.

Once in California, Gabe and Shannon find Peter who, with considerable effort, figures out Adam's codes and keys to how he laundered the money.

"The only respite they find is one afternoon in San Francisco where Shannon drives past Amelia's mansion and she sees her son on the lawn behind the iron fence playing with a puppy. Though the boy does not know her at all, Shannon stops the little puppy from escaping through the iron bars of the fence. Laird talks to Shannon, and for her, the reunion is overwhelmingly bittersweet as she realizes that Laird's disfigurement from the fire will always keep him from having a normal life. She realizes that she can only offer him a life on the run.

Amelia finds Shannon talking to Laird and is terrified that Shannon will tell the truth. Despite her hatred for Amelia, Shannon walks away, not disturbing Laird's life and his beliefs.

Shannon, Gabe, and Peter charter a plane to take them to Mexico. Peter is convinced they can recapture the stolen millions and live in Europe. However, Sardia and his fellow assassin, Joseph, kill the two pilots and board the plane as the real pilots. Over the ocean, a fight breaks out in which Gabe kills Joseph but is shot, and Shannon saves their lives by shooting Sardia.

They fly into Mexico and pay off the local *federales* to cut up the charter plane. They then rent a jet and chart a course fly to the Caribbean where they fuel up in Cayman. There they release the Swiss and Cayman bank accounts Adam Rivers had set up to hide the cartel's money.

On Cayman, Gabe and Shannon discover they have truly fallen in love. Peter is the best man at their wedding.

The End

APPENDIX C

List of Romance Publishers

Listed below are the names of the prominent romance publishers in the United States, Canada, and the United Kingdom. When available, we have listed the Web sites for these publishers, since many of them have their guidelines online.

Avalon Books
160 Madison Avenue
New York, NY 10016
Web site: *www.avalonbooks.com*

Avon Books
10 E. 53rd Street
New York, NY 10022
phone: (212) 207-7000
fax: (212) 207-7759
e-mail queries to avonromance@harpercollins.com

Ballantine Ivy
1745 Broadway, 18th Floor
New York, NY 10019
fax: (212) 940-7500
Web site: *www.ballantinebooks.com*

The Bantam Dell Publishing Group
1745 Broadway
New York, NY 10019

Barbour Publishing, Inc. & Heartsong Presents
P.O. Box 719
Uhrichsville, OH 44683
e-mail: fictionsubmit@barbourbooks.com; info@heartsongpresents.com

Belle Books
P.O. Box 67
Smyrna, GA 30081
e-mail: MossyEditorial@aol.com
Web site: *www.bellebooks.com*

Berkley Jove
375 Hudson Street
New York, NY 10014
phone: (212) 366-2000

BET Books/Arabesque
Office of the Publisher
555 West 57th Street, 11th Floor
New York, NY 10019
phone: (212) 975-1513
fax: (212) 975-1747
Web site: *www.bet.com* (look under the "books" section)

Dorchester Publishing
200 Madison Avenue, Suite 2000
New York, NY 10016
phone: (212) 725-8811
fax: (212) 532-1054

Ellora's Cave Publishing, Inc.
P.O. Box 787
Hudson, OH 44236-0787
e-mail: submissions@ellorascave.com

Genesis Press, Inc.
1213 Hwy. 45 North
Columbus, MS 39705
phone: (662) 329-9927
fax: (662) 329-9399
Web site: *www.genesis-press.com*

Harlequin Books—Canada
225 Duncan Mill Road
Don Mills, Ontario, Canada M3B3K9
phone: (416) 445-5860
fax: (416) 445-8655
Web site: *www.eharlequin.com*

Harlequin Mills & Boon Ltd.
United Kingdom
Eton House, 18-24 Paradise Road
Richmond, Surrey TW9 1SR
United Kingdom
phone: 011-44-020-8288-2800
fax: 011-44-020-8288-2898
Web site: *www.millsandboon.co.uk*

Harlequin Books—New York
233 Broadway
Suite 1001, 10th Floor
New York, NY 10279
phone: (212) 553-4200
fax: (212) 227-8669
Web site: *www.eharlequin.com*

Imajinn Books
P.O. Box 545
Canon City, CO 81215
phone: (877) 625-3592
e-mail: editors@imajinnbooks.com

High Country Publishers, Ltd.
197 New Market Center #135
Boone, NC 28607

Kensington Publishing Corp.
850 Third Avenue
New York, NY 10022
phone: (212) 407-1500
Web site: *www.kensingtonbooks.com*

Loveland Press, LLC
360 Logan Avenue
Loveland, CO 80537

LUNA Press
233 Broadway
Suite 1001, 10th Floor
New York, NY 10279
phone: (212) 553-4200
fax: (212) 227-8969

MIRA Books
225 Duncan Mill Road
Don Mills, Ontario, Canada M3B3K9
phone: (416) 445-5860
fax: (416) 445-8655
Web site: *www.eharlequinbooks.com*

Multnomah Publishers
204 W. Adams Avenue
P.O. Box 1720
Sisters, OR 97759
Web site: *www.multnomahbooks.com*

New American Library (NAL)
375 Hudson Street
New York, NY 10014
fax: (212) 366-2889

Pocket Books
1230 Avenue of the Americas
New York, NY 10020
fax: (212) 632-8084

Rainbow Books, Inc.
P.O. Box 430
Highland City, FL 33846-0430

Red Sage Publishing
P.O. Box 4844
Seminole, FL 33775

Silhouette Books
233 Broadway
Suite 1001, 10th Floor
New York, NY 10279
phone: (212) 533-4200
fax: (212) 227-8969
Web site: *www.eharlequinbooks.com*

St. Martin's Press
175 Fifth Avenue
New York, NY 10010

Steeple Hill
233 Broadway
Suite 1001, 10th Floor
New York, NY 10279
phone: (212) 553-4200
fax: (212) 227-8969
Web site: *www.eharlequinbooks.com*

Tor/Forge
Tom Doherty Associates, LLC
175 Fifth Avenue
New York, NY 10010
phone: (212) 388-0100

fax: (212) 388-0191
Web site: *www.tor.com*

Tyndale House Publishers, Inc.
351 Executive Drive
Carol Stream, IL 60188
Web site: *www.heartquest.com*

Warner Books
1271 Avenue of the Americas
New York, NY 10020
phone: (212) 522-7200
fax: (212) 522-7990

APPENDIX D

Recommended Resources

Here are some resources every romance writer should know about . . .

Magazines and Journals

ForeWord Magazine (*www.forewordmagazine.com*) is a bimonthly magazine that focuses on the achievements of independent publishers and their authors. Each issue includes book reviews, articles on market trends, industry information, and more.

Publishers Weekly (*www.publishersweekly.com*) is a weekly magazine that covers all the latest publishing industry news and gossip.

Romantic Times Magazine (*www.romantictimes.com*) is a magazine that reviews two hundred and fifty romances each month. Interesting and helpful articles on writing by published authors.

Books

Achity, Kenneth. *A Writer's Time*. New York: W. W. Norton & Co., 1995.

Ballon, Rachel. *Breathing Life into Your Characters*. Cincinnati: Writer's Digest Books, 2003.

Bartlett, John. *Bartlett's Familiar Quotations*. Boston: Little, Brown and Company, 1855, 1980.

Blanco, Jodee. *The Complete Guide to Book Publicity*. New York: Allworth Press, 2000.

Bowler, Peter. *The Superior Person's Book of Words*. New York: David R. Godine Publishers, 1986.

Daniel, Clifton, Editor in Chief. *Chronicle of the 20th Century*. New York: Chronicle Publications, 1987.

Florida, Richard. *The Rise of the Creative Class*. New York: Basic Books, 2003.

Garraty, John A. and Peter Gay. *The Columbia History of the World*. New York: Harper and Row, 1972.

Glennon, Lorraine, Editor in Chief. *Our Times, The Illustrated History of the 20th Century*. Atlanta: Turner Publishing, Inc., 1995.

Grun, Bernard. *The Timetables of History*. New York: Simon and Schuster, 1991.

Mayer, Bob. *The Novel Writer's Tool Kit*. Cincinnati: Writer's Digest Books, 2003.

McCutcheon, Mark. *The Writer's Guide to Everyday Life in the 1800s*. Cincinnati: Writer's Digest Books, 1993.

Popcorn, Faith. *Clicking*. New York: Harper Collins, 1996.

Rodale, J.I. *The Synonym Finder*. Emmaus, Pennsylvania: Warner Books, Rodale Press, Inc., 1986.

Thurman, Susan. *The Everything Grammar and Style Book*. Avon, Massachusetts: Adams Media Corporation, 2002.

Deluxe Hammond Medallion World Atlas, Webster Edition. Publishers United Guild, USA, 1986.

Yarwood, Doreen. *The Encyclopedia of World Costume*. New York: Macmillan Publishing, 1979.

Web Sites

Romance Writers of America, *www.rwanational.org*: This Web site is a must for all romance writers.

Forwriters.com, *www.forwriters.com*: This site gives geographical, historical, and scientific research.

Jaclyn Redings Useful Links for Romance Writers and Readers, *www.jaclynredings.com*: These are links for romance writers.

Literary Liaisons, *www.literaryliaisons.com*: These are resources for authors and readers of historical romance fiction.

Word Museum, *www.wordmuseum.com*: This site gives writing tools, including guidelines, classes, and services.

Harlequin Books; *www.eharlequin.com*: The most comprehensive publisher's Web site. This Web site also offers critiques of unpublished authors' work.

Organizations

Romance Writers of America
16000 Steubner Airline Hwy.
Suite 140
Spring, Texas 77379
Web site: *www.rwanational.org*

Conferences

The Romance Writers of America Conference; held annually

Romantic Times Magazine Convention; held annually

Contests and Awards

For Unpublished Writers

The Golden Heart Award, sponsored by Romance Writers of America (for unpublished authors)

For Published Authors

The RITA (sponsored by Romance Writers of America)

The Book of the Year Award—Romance (sponsored by *ForeWord Magazine*)

The Book of the Year Award—Romance (sponsored by Reader's Preference)

The Gold Medal Award (sponsored by *Romantic Times Magazine*)

Personal Letter to Aspiring Authors

Dear Reader:

My intent in writing this book and my hope for you is that you will find nuggets of guidance that will not only be valuable but will lead to your destiny of being published. However, there will still be questions I have not answered and issues I may not have addressed within these pages. I would truly like to help you or perhaps a family member who is struggling with the writing process. To that end, I have an e-mail address where you may contact me: angelwatchshow@hotmail.com. I answer my e-mails myself, and though there are times when I may get overwhelmed with mail, I will get to you. If you do not have e-mail you may write to me at: 2554 Lincoln Blvd. #295, Marina del Rey, CA 90291.

I wish each and every one of you the very best of luck with your writing. I support you in all your efforts. It is not an easy path you have chosen, but should you persevere, you will find joy in the writing itself, and that is profoundly exciting and rewarding.

Sincerely,
Catherine Lanigan

INDEX

hero
  in *The American President*, 31
  creation of, 30–34
  dialogue of, 69–70
  epiphany in, 26
  introduced, 50
  naming, 34
  physical makeup, 34–35
  testing of, by author, 35–36
  thoughts during love scene, 94, 95
  traits, 27–29
heroine
  classic, 40–41
  creation of, 43
  dialogue of, 68–69
  introduced, 50
  naming, 42
  physical makeup, 43–45
  psychic, 8
  testing of, by author, 45–46
  thoughts during love scene, 94, 95, 99
  traits, 38–40
historical periods, 11, 12, 13
historical romance, 11–13
  Civil war setting, 11
  historical periods in, 11, 12, 13
  paranormal in, 8
the historical "meet," 90–92
hook line, 111
hook paragraph, 112
HQN, 174

ImaJinn Books, 9
imprint lines, ix, 174
index cards, 57
inspiration, as gift from God, 186
inspirational, spiritual, and Christian
    romances, 9–10
Internet, 17
interviews
  preparation for, 19
  recording, 19
  as research tool, 18–20

Jackson, Peter, 7
Jenny, 8
Jung, Carl, 18

Keaton, Diane, 2
Kelly, Kitty, 18
Kensington Publishers, 13

kiss, 94, 99
Knight in Shining Armor (Devereaux), 7
Krantz, Judith, 102
Krentz, Jayne Anne, viii, 4, 178

Lanigan, Catherine
  address, 207
  *Angel Watch: Goosebumps, Signs, Dreams
      and Divine Nudges*, viii–ix, 18
  Beauty's Beast, 89–90
  Bound by Love, 68, 147
  California Moon, 135
  The Christmas Star, 59–60
  email address, 207
  personal letter to aspiring authors, 207
  A Promise Made, 19, 20
  Romancing the Stone, 26, 57
  Sins of Omission, 26
  Tender Malice, 63
  Wings of Destiny, 12, 21, 63, 78–79, 91
Lanigan, Dorothy, 16
Last Tango in Paris, 94
libraries and librarians, 17–18
licensing, of agents, 124
Little, Denise, 172, 176
Lord of the Rings, 7
love, 188–89
Love, Actually, 75
love at first sight, 86–87
love scene, 93–99
  action after lovemaking, 94, 95
  dialogue, 95, 96, 97
  heroine's thoughts during, 95
  hero's thoughts during, 95
  kiss in, 94, 99
  proposition of sex, 95
  sexual act in, 95
  vocabulary, 73
Love Story (Segal), 30
Lumet, Sydney, 174

Macomber, Debbie, 178
magazines,
  as research tools, 22–23
  for romance novelists, 203
mainstream romance
  audience for, 6
  category romance v., 4
  parameters for, 6
  thriller format's acceptance as, 6
  trade paperbacks and, ix

Books from Allworth Press

Allworth Press is an imprint of Allworth Communications, Inc. Selected titles are listed below.

The Author's Toolkit: A Step-by-Step Guide to Writing and Publishing Your Book, Revised Edition
by Mary Embree (paperback, 5 ½ × 8 ½, 192 pages, $16.95)

The Writer's Legal Guide: An Author's Guild Desk Reference, Third Edition
by Tad Crawford and Kay Murray (paperback, 6 × 9, 320 pages, $19.95)

The Complete Guide to Book Publicity, Second Edition
by Jodee Blanco (paperback, 6 × 9, 304 pages, $19.95)

The Complete Guide to Book Marketing, Revised Edition
by David Cole (paperback, 6 × 9, 256 pages, $19.95)

The Copyright Guide: A Friendly Handbook to Protecting and Profiting from Copyrights, Third Edition
by Lee Wilson (paperback, 6 × 9, 256 pages, $19.95)

The Writer's Guide to Queries, Pitches & Proposals
by Moira Allen (paperback, 6 × 9, 288 pages, $16.95)

Making Crime Pay: The Writer's Guide to Criminal Law, Evidence, and Procedure
by Andrea Campbell (paperback, 6 × 9, 304 pages, $19.95)

Starting Your Career as a Freelance Writer
by Moira Anderson Allen (paperback, 6 × 9, 272 pages, $19.95)

Successful Syndication: A Guide for Writers and Cartoonists
by Michael Sedge (paperback, 6 × 9, 176 pages, $16.95)

Business and Legal Forms for Authors and Self-Publishers, Third Edition
by Tad Crawford (paperback, 8 3/8 × 10 7/8, 160 pages, $29.95)

Fair Use, Free Use, and Use by Permission: How to Handle Copyrights in All Media
by Lee Wilson (paperback, 6 × 9, 256 pages, $24.95)

Please write to request our free catalog. To order by credit card, call 1-800-491-2808 or send a check or money order to Allworth Press, 10 East 23rd Street, Suite 510, New York, NY 10010. Include $6 for shipping and handling for the first book ordered and $1 for each additional book. Eleven dollars plus $1 for each additional book if ordering from Canada. New York State residents must add sales tax.

To see our complete catalog on the World Wide Web, or to order online, you can find us at **www.allworth.com.**